PARENTS

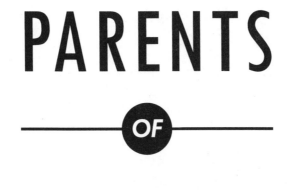

OF

MISSIONARIES

PARENTS

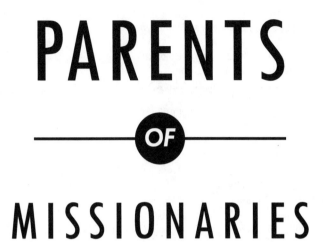

OF

MISSIONARIES

How to thrive and stay
connected when your children
and grandchildren serve cross-culturally

Cheryl Savageau, EdD and Diane Stortz

COLORADO SPRINGS • MILTON KEYNES • HYDERABAD

Authentic Publishing
We welcome your questions and comments.

USA   1820 Jet Stream Drive, Colorado Springs, CO 80921
       www.authenticbooks.com
UK   9 Holdom Avenue, Bletchley, Milton Keynes, Bucks, MK1 1QR
       www.authenticmedia.co.uk
India Logos Bhavan, Medchal Road, Jeedimetla Village, Secunderabad
       500 055, A.P.

Parents of Missionaries
ISBN-13: 978-1-934068-39-7
ISBN-10: 1-934068-39-X

10 09 08 / 6 5 4 3 2 1

A catalog record for this book is available from the Library of Congress.

Cover and interior design: projectluz.com
Editorial team: KJ Larson, Dana Bromley, Michaela Dodd

Printed in the United States of America

We do not often think about the families missionaries leave behind, yet parents of missionaries often miss their children and grandchildren and experience a variety of emotions: fear, anger, pride, loneliness, and perhaps even bitterness toward God. Authors Cheryl Savageau and Diane Stortz are uniquely qualified to address these important but often neglected topics, providing tangible steps toward acceptance and adjustment.

Doug Priest
executive director, CMF International

This book speaks to the greatest unseen cost of missionary work—the ache of parents separated from their children and grandchildren who serve Christ overseas.

Dick Alexander
senior minister, LifeSpring Christian Church, Cincinnati, Ohio

Just enough gripping stories and quotes from parents of missionaries and their missionary offspring humanize this handbook that deals with God's call to be loving parents of missionaries who build healthy family relationships. I recommend it also for church leaders who want to better understand the dynamics of sending out missionary families from their church.

Dr. Wayne Shaw
dean emeritus and professor of preaching, Lincoln Christian College and Seminary, Lincoln, Illinois; president of the board, Asian Pacific Christian Mission International; and a POM

Parents of Missionaries lets parents know they aren't alone in their thoughts and feelings and provides practical suggestions for dealing with them. A wonderful gift for missionaries to give to their parents, especially those [missionaries] leaving for the first time. Agencies may also want to give it to parents of new missionaries.

Dr. Ronald L. Koteskey
member care consultant, New Hope International Ministries

As the missions minister at our church, I plan to buy a copy for each of the families whose children are called to be missionaries.

Wade Landers
missions minister, College Heights Christian Church, Joplin, Missouri

This is a must-read. I know of no other book that so expertly addresses the needs of parents of missionaries at so many levels.

Sherrie Johnson
ENHANCE Dept., coordinator of Family Ministries, EFCA ReachGlobal

The authors of this book have written from personal experience and given a gift to everyone involved in supporting a missionary. The comprehensive treatment of the challenges that must be faced and the practical helps they have provided will both comfort and equip families who are sending someone they love to "the uttermost parts of the earth" in the name of Christ.

Cam Huxford
senior pastor, Savannah Christian Church, Savannah, Georgia

This comprehensive tool will help parents become missionaries most enthusiastic cheerleaders. *Parents of Missionaries* is packed full of insights about our God-given emotions that make it difficult to release our children to live in a distant land. But by being a supportive parent, we can encourage them to persevere in the role God has called them. We, too, will share in the joy of the harvest!

Lorrie Lindgren
CEO and president of Women of the Harvest

Most of us find it a lot easier to write a check than to face prolonged separation from our loved ones. This book will help all of us with loved ones involved in cross-cultural ministry to make sure our relationships survive and thrive. Thanks to Cheryl and Diane for showing how we can support our children when they follow God's call—even when fulfilling the Great Commission takes them to the other side of the world.

Dr. David Faust
president, Cincinnati Christian University

Real stories and honest emotions from POMs and their missionary children give us insight into the struggles of both parties. Diane and Cheryl give practical, positive advice. POMs cannot help but be encouraged after reading this book. We can't wait to share this book with every one of our POMs.

Steve and Becky Overlin
Pioneer Bible Translators Missionary Care Dept., Ministering to POMs,
their missionary children, and grandchildren

A book for parents of missionaries . . . what a needed resource! Cheryl Savageau and Diane Stortz do an outstanding job of helping POMs honestly deal with all the complex emotions involved in this journey of change, pain, and fulfillment.

Dave Stone
senior minister, Southeast Christian Church, Louisville, Kentucky

What is the hidden cost in the lives of those who release their children and grandchildren to the Lord's service? And, just as important, how can family members transform themselves from reluctant observers into powerful participants? *Parents of Missionaries* will help every missionary-sending family navigate this challenging and potential packed journey.

Steve Richardson
president, Pioneers-USA, Orlando, Florida

I wish this book had been around as my husband and I headed to the mission field with our young children! I plan to adopt it as required reading for a class I teach. This beautiful, much needed book will help its readers stay connected with their children and grandchildren in a meaningful way for life.

Dr. Linda F. Whitmer
professor of inter-cultural studies, Pacific Christian College of Hope International University, Fullerton, California

A much-needed tool to help that oft-overlooked population, parents sending children and grandchildren off to the far corners of the globe.

Connie Blake
director of debriefing and renewal, Mission Training International

It is strange how there will be days, like today,

when my heart yearns to see my son.

Little things . . . will bring tears to my eyes.

It is an honor to be a parent of a missionary,

but it's also sometimes hard.

—Bonnie

When someone learns that your kids and/or grandkids are on the foreign mission field, and they say something akin to "Oh, I don't know *how* you can stand that!"—Rule #1 is don't hit them! Instead, pull out your ever-ready photos of your family and say how proud you are of your children and that you are looking forward to rejoicing with them in heaven on that day described in Revelation 7:9–10.

After this I looked and there before me was a

great multitude that no one could count, from

every nation, tribe, people and language, standing

before the throne and in front of the Lamb. They

were wearing white robes and were holding palm

branches in their hands. And they cried out in a

loud voice: "Salvation belongs to our God, who

sits on the throne, and to the Lamb" (NIV).

—Susan

Dedicated to Jim Penny, 1934–2006
and
Connie Phipps Young, 1930–2008,
Greater Cincinnati Area Parents of Missionaries

Contents

CAN I TELL YOU HOW I FEEL?
POMs can adjust and thrive by honestly dealing with four key life-issues.

HELLO, GOOD-BYE; HELLO, GOOD-BYE

POMs can meet the challenges of preparation, send-off, understanding life on the field, and reconnecting at furlough time.

STAYING CONNECTED

Practical, inspirational insights for creating and keeping strong family bonds across the miles.

FROM SURVIVING TO THRIVING
The POM journey can lead to good places, if we are willing.

WHERE THE JOURNEY BEGINS

●

———————————————

Families matter to God; the Bible makes this clear. God created us to live in relationship with Him and other people. He puts us in families at the beginning of life so we can have a safe place to learn about trust, community, and grace. He wants loving parents to help children understand the nature of His love.

Jesus said we shouldn't love anyone (or anything) more than we love Him. Strong family ties should not keep anyone from following God's will. But Jesus did not teach us to stop caring about family as we follow Him. If He has called our sons and daughters into missions, by all means, they should go; we must send them. But we should not feel guilty about missing our children and grandchildren when they are gone. We don't stop being a family. We can stay connected, and we honor God when we do. He's the one, after all, who stopped at nothing to stay connected to us.

Life in general and parenthood in particular come with many experiences that cause worry and pain, but parents whose adult children enter long-term missions work endure a unique set of stressors that often go unrecognized. Consequently, while much of what we write in this book can be generalized and applied

1

to other life situations, our particular focus involves the special experiences of parents of missionaries (POMs).

Again and again, we see missionaries hungry for their parents' blessing on their work and parents struggling to cope with the onslaught of emotions and life changes that come with having a missionary son or daughter. The family of God must find the heart to minister to hurting families left behind, to share their burden and empower them to give their blessing and fulfill their role as senders.

We offer this book as a tool for that purpose. We want to help POMs survive their period of adjustment and thrive as they take their place in God's plan. We want to help families stay strong and connected, even when they are separated for the cause of world missions.

We know individual reactions to becoming a POM vary; one size does not fit all. Some POMs struggle profoundly, others less so. You will find yourself somewhere on that spectrum.

We also recognize that not all POMs share our faith in Christ. Christian or not, the issues are the same. Those of a different faith persuasion may have more difficulty understanding why their son or daughter wants to serve in missions, but many readily support their child's desire to do good. If you do not follow Jesus, please don't put this book down. It can help you know how to stay connected to your family living on the mission field.

If you are a veteran POM, reading this book may prompt regret about how some matters were handled in your family. If this happens, don't despair. Instead, use the information provided to strengthen tattered bonds or to start over.

Last, while we recognize that siblings of missionaries experience many of the same emotions as POMs, we've chosen to limit this book to the experience of parents. We also realize that most POMs consider their missionary's spouse as one of their own children, but for simplicity we refer mainly to "your missionary" throughout the book.

Unless otherwise noted, all quotes from POMs or missionaries came to us directly through our website, research, or personal conversations or e-mails. In many cases we have changed or omitted names to preserve privacy.

Without a doubt, God does ask parents and children (and grandchildren) to separate when He calls missionaries into His service. Still, we strongly believe the good work of proclaiming the gospel and making disciples was not meant to eclipse the loving family bonds God ordained.

The POM experience amounts to a journey through change, pain, and adjustment. Wherever you are on that journey, our prayer for you is that reading this book will encourage you and help you thrive and stay connected with your children and grandchildren overseas.

—*Cheryl Savageau, Greenville, South Carolina*
—*Diane Stortz, Cincinnati, Ohio*
January 2008

THIS ISN'T EASY

---①---

God's Call to Parents of Missionaries

I put my son and daughter-in-law on the plane yesterday morning for a four-year commitment to East Asia. I'm struggling with losing my best friend.

—a POM dad

Keith and Lorraine sigh and smile as the jet pulls away from the gate at the Kiev airport. The two weeks they spent with their daughter's family on the mission field in Ukraine have been two of the best weeks of their lives. Seeing where their daughter and her husband and two children are living, getting to know the other missionaries on the team, and meeting the people the team works with—what a tremendous blessing the trip has been! And two uninterrupted weeks to enjoy their wonderful grandchildren—and take so many pictures! Keith and Lorraine are proud of their daughter and the work she does with her family. They feel even more invested in the work now that they've seen it in person. But both are wondering, as the jet soars into the air, *How long will it be before we see them again?* Keith takes Lorraine's hand. He knows what she is thinking. He is thinking the same thing. *This isn't easy.*

It's Christmas at Roberta and Bob's house. Roberta's niece has come to spend the day, along with Bob's sister, her husband, and their young son, Jack. Roberta and Bob's own son, Troy, left for the mission field earlier in the year with his wife and two-year-old daughter; this Christmas is Roberta and Bob's first time to be apart from Troy and his family for the holidays. Four-year-old Jack keeps everyone smiling and laughing most of the day, but after dinner, when Roberta and Bob take time to open the gifts from Troy and his family, Roberta begins to cry. Long minutes pass before her sobbing stops, although everyone tries to console her, even Jack. "Sorry, everyone," she says, trying to smile as she grabs a tissue to dry her face. She wonders how many more Christmases like this they will have, and she thinks, *This isn't easy.*

The sorting and packing and shipping are done. Departure day has arrived. Parents Lynn and Mark are stoic as they join their daughter, Heidi, and her husband, Jared, for breakfast at a pancake house, along with Heidi's sister, Kristen. Their minister and a few close friends also have come to say good-bye. There are hugs and prayers and tears when the meal is over, then silence, interrupted by small talk, takes over on the way to the airport. Lynn, Mark, and Kristen watch silently as Heidi and Jared check their bags. Then, "Well, Mom, Dad, I guess this is it." More hugs, more tears. "You know we love you," Mark says. "E-mail or call us as soon as you can." Heidi and Jared walk close together toward security. Heidi turns once to wave, and then they are gone. Kristen begins to wail, suddenly too overcome with sorrow to be embarrassed. Mark pulls out his handkerchief and hands it to Kristen, and Lynn prays, *God, help us, please. This isn't easy.*

Their son's voice over the speaker phone is full of joy. "Mom, Dad, there's something I want to share with you. Laura and I think God is calling us to work as missionaries in Asia. We've been praying about this for a while now. Isn't it exciting! What do you think?"

Tom and his wife, Rachel, exchange startled looks. Rachel clears her throat. "Well, honey, that's big news. Our family has always tried to share our faith with others." Tom is staring at the phone, thinking, *Missionaries? Asia? That's pretty far away. Isn't it dangerous over there? Leave us? This is what God wants? What about your law career? God, this isn't easy!*

When God invites a son or daughter into missions, He also invites the parents. For some parents of missionaries (POMs), the invitation from God is somewhat expected. Some POMs were missionaries themselves and raised their children on the mission field. Other POMs heard from their children early on that they wanted to be missionaries. Still others lead or attend churches with a strong missions focus that captured the heart of their children. For other parents, God's invitation is a complete surprise. Whatever your circumstances, it's likely the invitation you received from God sounded something like this:

"Your child will travel more and live farther from you than you ever expected. He'll learn a language you don't speak and eat foods that are strange to you. Your grandchildren will grow up calling another country home; you won't get to see them very often.

"Your child and his family will be away for months or years at a time; they'll miss birthdays and graduations and holidays with you; they won't be around when nieces and nephews are born or when aunts and uncles die or when you're old and needing help at home.

"Your child is doing this because he loves me and because I've asked him to do it. Please let him go with your blessing and support. I know you will miss your child and your grandchildren, and I'll make sure you don't have to face all this alone. I'll connect you with others who can help, and I will be with you always. I promise you it won't be easy, but I also promise you joy."

If you're a POM, even if your child is still preparing for the mission field or just considering it, that's your invitation: Let go. Send your child with your blessing and your support. Connect with God and with others who are doing the same thing, so you can encourage one another. I (Diane) was a POM, and I can tell you, this isn't easy! But I can also tell you that it is worth it, and it brings joy.

Do you have conflicted feelings about this role you're invited to assume? There's no one-size-fits-all reaction, but most POMs do experience both joy and sorrow at the prospect, or the reality, of sending a child overseas as a missionary. If you are like most POMs, however, you have tried not to admit to this conflict. You may have put on a brave face in the church hallway and said, "Yes, we're very proud"; then you shut the door behind you at home and wept. (Or perhaps you sat in stony silence if you're a man.) Or maybe you've argued with your daughter about the ten reasons she should not become a missionary, but not one of them is the real reason, which is "I'll miss you." Or you are extremely happy to think about your son introducing people to Jesus but can't understand what's wrong with your faith. And something must be wrong because you don't know how you are going to stand it when he and his wife and your only grandchildren say good-bye and leave you standing alone at the airport. A real Christian wouldn't be fazed by that, right?

Parents of missionaries have not always had the support and encouragement they need, but that is beginning to change. Cheryl and I pray this book gives you comfort, understanding, direction, and joy as you move forward on the POM path. Our Father's invitation to parents of missionaries is not always easy to accept, but it can influence and enrich our lives in wonderful ways.

Few of us were perfect parents, but somehow we taught our children to love God, and the hearts of our children have become hearts that God can use. Realize, then, that God has been calling you to be a POM and using you all along. God will continue to use you now and provide what you need to thrive as you answer His invitation to let go, to bless your missionary to do this important, life-giving work, and to seek and give encouragement by connecting with God and with others.

Let Go

The first part of God's invitation, letting go, has several layers, each equally important, although POMs may have more difficulty with one than another.

Expectations for the Future

The first layer is letting go of our expectations for the future. Children grow up and begin to lead their own lives as productive adults, and this is what we want for them. Still, many of us look forward to sharing special times together on a regular basis, maybe even living close enough to have frequent contact. Does your best friend get to meet her daughter for lunch once a week? Does your co-worker see her grandchildren every weekend? Does your neighbor play golf with his son twice a month? Even if your daughter has known since she was twelve that she wanted to be a missionary, there are cultural expectations for parents' relationships with adult children, and we can't entirely escape being molded by them. But we must let them go.

Sometimes the announcement that our children will be missionaries comes at a time in our lives when we are unsettled, unsure of what our future holds. A job layoff, a serious illness, divorce or widowhood, an empty nest, marriage difficulties, retirement, moving—life shifts, and disruptions like these affect our sense of stability and security. And now our daughter and her family are going to be missionaries in Tanzania? No matter how supportive we want to be, if our own stability and security are already compromised by our circumstances, we may not hear our daughter's news as tidings of great joy. We know in our heads what the Bible says about God taking care of us and all our needs; we know it in our hearts if we've allowed ourselves to experience it in the past. But our human nature wants to be in control, and we do not want to let go.

Concerns and Worries

A second kind of letting go involves concerns and worries for our children's well-being. We may question the wisdom of a child's decision to be a missionary. Parents who don't share their child's faith may especially struggle with this, but even Christian parents can question the certainty of God's call as well as the timing and location of where their child is headed. Years of college, graduate degrees—is all that going to be wasted? What about future financial security? How will our son or daughter or our grandchildren get medical care? What is the political climate in the region where our missionary will serve? Are Christians welcome? Will our son or daughter face danger or persecution?

Relationship Fears

Hardest of all, however, when we think about letting go, is

letting go of our fears about our relationship with our children and grandchildren. We can be afraid that our relationship will lose closeness—what if the emotional bond between us can't withstand the distance? Or maybe the emotional bond between us has been tenuous at best, with unresolved conflicts from adolescence and early adulthood swept under the rug and lying there, unaddressed and unforgiven. How will we ever address those issues and reconnect when we're thousands of miles apart? How will we get to know our grandchildren? POMs need to know that they can create and maintain a close emotional bond with adult children and grandchildren serving cross-culturally. We're writing this book to help you do exactly that!

Give Your Blessing

Children of all ages desire to be highly valued and accepted by their parents. In the early 1990s, John Trent and Gary Smalley wrote *The Blessing*, in which they explain this important phenomenon and describe ways parents can give their children their blessing. They also write about the devastation experienced by those who never receive their parents' unconditional love and blessing. Based on their research, Trent and Smalley define the blessing this way: "A family blessing begins with *meaningful touching*. It continues with a *spoken message* of *high value,* a message that pictures a *special future* for the individual being blessed, and one that is based on an *active commitment* to see the blessing come to pass."[1]

What does it mean to give your blessing to your child's

decision to be a missionary? Does it mean squelching your fears and concerns, stuffing them down, putting on a brave face, and pretending that everything is okay? Fortunately, no!

Accept Your Child as Separate

What blessing does mean, first, is accepting your child as an adult, separate from you, with his or her own talents, interests, skills, and dreams. The future your child is seeking may not be the future you had picked for him, but it is his future, a *special future*. My daughter Sheila is a gifted vocalist and performer. I always expected her to pursue a career in musical theater or contemporary Christian music. When she chose missions, I wondered what would happen to her music.

Sheila believed that if she was willing to give up her music, God would give it back to her, and He did! Soon after her arrival on the field, she became the lead singer of an all-girl alternative rock band. The band performed in cafés and clubs, cut a few singles that got radio play, and won fourth place and "Best Young Band" in a competition with a hundred other bands from all over eastern Europe. Besides leading to some meaningful friendships, the band was a perfect vehicle for Sheila and her husband to be introduced to dozens of young adults in their city.

Still, I harbored disappointment that Sheila wasn't performing full-time, and I suspected she knew I felt this way. So one day when she was home on furlough, I took her out to lunch. "I want you to know," I said, "that I'm sorry for ever making you feel that your music was more important to me than you are." Instantly Sheila's eyes filled with tears, and I knew in that moment I gave, and she received, my blessing.

Giving your blessing also means being willing to accept the changes that your missionary's work brings into your own life, even though it is difficult at times. Letting your missionary know that you are "with him" or "with her," despite the personal cost, communicates high value and active commitment.

Communicate Support

We also convey our blessing when we find ways to assure our missionary of our love and support in ways that are meaningful to him or her. Dan found it hard to listen to his daughter talk about her missionary plans. He became distraught, and she became defensive. Wanting to find a way to express his feelings without seeming a threat, Dan wrote his daughter a letter.

In the letter, Dan assured his daughter of his love and his support for her plans. He apologized for reacting in unhelpful ways and let her know that he was beginning to work on his own issues. He offered to simply listen the next time they talked and volunteered to help with preparation plans. Later, Dan told a friend that his daughter had thanked him twice for the letter. "I can tell it meant a lot to her," he said. "Things have improved, and for that we are thankful."

Volunteering to help with packing and other departure preparations; staying in touch through e-mail, phone calls, and packages; visiting on the field; finding ways to become involved in the mission work itself—these are a few ways you might powerfully communicate support. My daughter enjoyed receiving cards in her mailbox on special days, just as she would if she lived here. Ask questions about your missionary's field of service, the people he is meeting, and the challenges and joys he is experiencing—and pray. Some parents become forwarding agents or prayer mobilizers.

Giving our blessing is more than a one-time event. Probably the most difficult circumstance in which we offer our blessing is when we're in ill health. One missionary had this experience: "The last time I hugged my mother good-bye, we both knew she was terminally ill and that I would not be with her when she died. She must have understood my feelings because she said, 'Rose, it's okay. I think it is wonderful that we know ahead of time we won't see each other again. This way we haven't left anything unsaid between us.' Her reassurance that I was doing the right thing was her parting gift to me."[2]

Blessing your missionary and his or her work may not always be easy to do, but it is critical. Giving your blessing may be the most powerful thing you can do to allow your missionary to feel a close emotional connection with you despite the miles.

Connect with God and Others

God invites POMs to connect with Him and with others who understand.

Connect with God

Thinking about God being separated from Jesus when He was an infant in a stable, far from His heavenly throne, and when His bruised and beaten body hung on a cross to pay for my sins, reminds me that God understood that I missed my daughter when she served Him in another part of the world.

We read in Romans 11 and 12 that because of God's mercy we should consider our bodies as living sacrifices and that our actions should flow out of that. One action POMs can do daily is give to God our desire for more time and interaction with our missionary sons and daughters and our grandchildren. God doesn't overlook this sacrifice; He intends to repay us! Jesus said that everyone who has given up "houses or brothers or sisters or father or mother or children or property" for His sake will receive "a hundred times as much in return" (Matthew 19:29 NLT). I don't believe Jesus was thinking only of missionaries when He said this.

God's love for us is deep and personal. He delights in the details of our lives. He understands how we think and what we feel. His Holy Spirit is our comforter, and His Son is our strength. It's important for us as POMs to nurture an intimate connection with God, allowing Him to sustain us through the years apart from our missionary children. At the same time, we need to remember that God also works for our benefit through other believers. We gain strength as well as give it to others when we "carry each other's burdens, and in this way . . . fulfill the law of Christ" (Galatians 6:2 NIV).

Connect with Others

When we connect with other POMs, we discover we're not alone in how we feel. We are not the only ones wondering what is wrong with our faith because we grieve our missionary being so far away; other POMs have felt like this too. We are encouraged by the vitality of those who have been POMs for years and who, with tears in their eyes, say they wouldn't have it any other way, because although it hasn't been easy, God is good.

Encouraging ourselves by connecting with others shows our missionary we are entering in and we will be okay. This doesn't absolve missionaries of their responsibilities to their parents, but it does help them feel that their parents are actively working with them in this new kind of life God has called us to.

Reading this book is a good step toward connecting. Getting on a newsletter list, finding another POM to correspond with, starting a POM group for fellowship and learning—all are ways to connect and get support for ourselves as well as offer it to others.

A Process in Stages

Being the parent of a missionary will never be easy, but it becomes easier. It will not always be joyful, but it becomes a joy. You can thrive as a POM and stay connected to your children and grandchildren throughout their years overseas. You are likely to find that your adjustment to life as a POM develops by stages.

Preparation and Departure

The time leading up to a missionary's first departure can be difficult. One POM said that the turmoil before her son left for the field was "actually worse than the separation itself." In the beginning, you may wrestle with fears and doubts. You start looking for answers to your questions, you dialog with your missionary about your concerns, you look within and determine that you can and will give your blessing to your missionary to pursue his or her call.

You decide to get support for yourself. You connect with God and with others and deal with your grief. You do all you can to create a healthy adult-to-adult relationship with your child. You participate in preparations and in your missionary's send-off and departure.

On the Field

Your missionary moves to the field and settles in; you establish communication, receiving photos, e-mails, and phone calls. You become more knowledgeable about the field and the work your child is doing, and you begin to find ways to be part of it. You may even travel to the field to visit and experience your missionary's new life close up.

Long Term

You welcome your missionary back on furlough and send her off again. But your relationship with her is secure, and the communication between you is good. Your relationship with your grandchildren is deepening too, and they look forward to visiting you as a stability point in a country that is not really home to them.

Although there are times when you miss your missionary intensely, you know that he is happy and fulfilled. You know that in heaven you will meet people who are there because of your missionary, and that thought is deeply satisfying.

Your relationship with God is stronger than ever, and you've connected with other POMs who have become some of your best friends. You have increased both your awareness of the needs of the world around you and your interest in missions. You even find that you're glad to be the parent of a missionary! That's the day you know you've begun to thrive as a POM.

CAN I TELL YOU HOW I FEEL?

POMs can adjust and thrive by honestly dealing with four key life-issues.

SOMETHING MUST BE WRONG WITH ME

2

The Experience of Loss

I felt we were losing them, and it seemed like it would be a permanent loss. I've never felt a deeper sadness that I couldn't fully express to anyone.

—a POM mom

Perhaps you know Martha, or somebody very much like her. At fifty-six, Martha lives in the Bible Belt state of Indiana with her husband, Ron. They have two married sons living out-of-state and a daughter, Angela, who alternates between living at home and on campus at a nearby Christian college.

While on Christmas break last year, Angela startled Ron and Martha by announcing she and her fiancé, Jeremy, planned to become foreign missionaries after their college graduation in the spring. She explained that months of praying together and with professors helped them feel sure God wanted them to work long-term with an unreached people group in Africa.

A flood of conflicting emotions besieged Martha after she heard Angela's news. She felt happy that Angela had chosen such a capable, Christian young man for her life partner. But although Martha and Ron believed in world missions and supported missionaries through their church, Martha did not feel entirely happy about her daughter's plans to become one. She had not expected it! She felt surprised and hurt that Angela had made this important career decision without bringing Martha into the loop.

With two sons already living some distance away, Martha hoped her daughter would stay close to home. She looked forward with happy anticipation to becoming a grandparent, and she wanted to live near her grandchildren and enjoy frequent contact with them. She hoped to babysit and to attend games, recitals, and school activities. Martha wanted to help Angela navigate the challenges of adulthood and parenthood.

At first, Martha attributed her swirling emotions to holiday fatigue. She hoped the restful quiet of January would help her feel better, but as the weeks and months passed she continued to feel distressed without understanding why. She tried to ignore her feelings of anxiety, fear, and sadness and told herself that in the end Angela would probably change her mind anyway; the Angela she knew would not feel content living in a hut without plumbing!

Martha kept herself busy and chose not to tell anyone about her thoughts and feelings. She experienced profound self-doubt and feared others would take a critical view if they knew of her inner struggle. She believed having an adult child enter missions would not upset a real Christian.

As Angela's graduation grew near, Martha could no longer keep a lid on her feelings. She feared she might come unglued. The pressure inside her increased until she broke down and shared her struggle with a safe, caring friend. "I just feel irritable," she confided. "I cry easily and often. I get mad when people at church congratulate me about Angela's decision to become a missionary. Ron and I squabble over the smallest things. I don't sleep well anymore, and I catch too many colds. I appreciate that Angela and Jeremy want to dedicate their lives to Christian service, but I don't feel happy about their plans to move so far away. For the longest time, I've been afraid to share my feelings with anyone else. I feel selfish and question my own love of God. I should feel happy because our daughter wants to live out her commitment to God in a serious way! Why am I having so much trouble? Is something wrong with me?"

Martha asked a difficult question. Much of her distress reflects the natural grief connected with the very real losses she will suffer because of Angela's decision. However, some of her distress stems from other issues in her life that need attention. Martha will learn more about these as she works through her time of crisis and begins a journey toward personal growth. Her feelings will become easier to understand later in this chapter when we consider them against the backdrop of her personal history, life circumstances, and way of thinking. At this point, however, I (Cheryl) want to focus attention on the matter of POM grief.

Facing the Reality of POM Grief

Not everyone finds POM grief easy to understand. However, we have come to recognize that grief among parents of missionaries is widespread and a serious problem. We often hear statements like "I've never felt a deeper sadness"; "My husband and I feel lonely, alienated, and shocked"; "I've grieved over her leaving from the time she decided to go."

Most POMs respond with gratitude when we recognize and validate their pain. They seem relieved when someone else "gets it." POMs have told us, "The word that really hits home is *grieving*"; "It really helps validate my emotions when you zero in on grief"; "What popped out at me was the word *grief*—a label for what I feel!"

Reactions Do Vary

Not all POMs react the same way to learning their adult children will become missionaries. One recruit who experienced such differences wrote, "My husband's parents applauded . . . and supported our decision. My mother exploded!" Some POMs apparently don't struggle much; others struggle but minimize or deny their pain. We know many others grieve openly and intensely.

Each type of reaction should enjoy respect. We need to refrain from judging the way others feel. Doing so only causes hurt, and it doesn't make sense to judge feelings because feelings result from an involuntary and amoral process. Emotions do not reflect character. They are the product of a series of complex interactions of the forces working within us, around us, and from our past. Because emotions emerge from such a complex process, they can seem hard to understand at first. We usually have to unpack emotions, or identify the underlying forces that drive them, before they make sense.

We know POMs react more negatively to an adult child entering missions when the news comes as a surprise. One mom caught off guard recounted, "My daughter never told me she had been called as a child to missions. I never knew she'd even thought about it, let alone felt called. . . . How can I support a calling that was never part of [her life]?" Another reported, "We are still reeling from finding out that our son and daughter-in-law plan to move away from their family permanently. [Our son] . . . was less than candid with us . . . because he feared we'd go ballistic."

It's Not about Faith

POM grief stems from an inability to change unpleasant realities. Parents know they will miss the presence of their missionary and grandchildren and that their child will miss opportunities for a more lucrative career and safer living conditions. POMs must surrender both their ambitions for their child's future and their hopes of living close enough to share life and help out in emergencies. POMs also grieve because normal life gets put on hold while they struggle to move through the stages of adjustment.

POM grief does not reflect a lack of faith or personal weakness. Strength, pain, and faith can coexist, as this statement by a

POM shows: "I never used to cry easily, so my children usually didn't see me cry. But I just couldn't hold back the tears sometimes. I finally told my son that he might see me crying at times but not to let that stop him from following God's call on his life. It was a blessing to watch him face his sending committee and hear how grounded he was in his faith." Parents simply find it hard to let their children and grandchildren go far away. Rhonda shared, "When they left for training, their leaving permanently became a reality, and it really hit hard."

A Reason for Discomfort?

Some within the church community have expressed discomfort with our focus on POM grief. One workshop attendee asked, "What's the big deal? It's not like they're dead!" while another said, "Having a child enter missions isn't as bad as having a child outside the faith." A few missions-minded people have blatantly objected to our focus on this issue and argued that only joy should abound when young people choose a career in missions. Curious others have honestly asked how POM grief differs from whining.

Please stop now to assess your reaction to our assertion that POM grief exists as a serious and neglected problem. If you don't understand why we think so, the following discussion may help you. If you partially understand, perhaps your grasp of this important matter will be enhanced.

Understanding Grief

We can better understand the phenomenon of POM grief in particular once we understand grief in general. Consequently, we'll review some basic facts about grief before devoting more time to understanding Martha's grief.

What Causes Grief?

Grief occurs in response to loss. People most often associate grief with bereavement, or loss of a loved one through death, but it also occurs with many other kinds of losses. Grief may emerge due to loss of a spouse, family member, or friend; the prospect of an empty nest; alienation within a family; or losing employment, social status, social roles, a home, or a favorite place. It may follow an experience with war, violence, or injustice or loss of health, body parts, ability, trust, innocence, prized possessions, or pets.

Does Grieving Reflect Weakness?

Absolutely not! Grief cannot indicate weakness because the Bible teaches that God grieves (Genesis 6:6) and describes Jesus as a man acquainted with grief (Isaiah 53:3). Since God created us to grieve, we should not fear the process, feel ashamed of our grief, or run from it. We should not criticize others who grieve.

What Purpose Does Grief Serve?

Grief helps us confront and deal with life's unwelcome realities. An active, healthy grieving process enables us to face the pain and disorientation brought on by loss and to move toward positive change and personal growth. Well-managed grief ends in personal transformation.

What Does Grief Look Like?

The intensity of grief can range from mild to crippling. It can make us feel crazy. We associate grief with emotional sorrow, but it also manifests as mental anguish, behavioral disturbances, physical complaints, social problems, and spiritual unrest.

Emotional Symptoms. Initial feelings triggered by loss may include shock, disbelief, or numbness. Later, feelings of sadness, despair, loneliness, abandonment, yearning, fear, anxiety, helplessness, hopelessness, fatigue, anger, frustration, or self-blame may arise.

Mental Symptoms. Grief can affect our capacity to think clearly. It may cause poor concentration, mental disorganization, mental fog, distorted memories, hypervigilance, or even thoughts of suicide.

Behavioral Symptoms. We sometimes "act out" grief in hopes of avoiding emotional pain. Acting-out grief symptoms can include excessive eating, sleeping, working, spending, playing, or substance abuse.

Physical Symptoms. Grief may cause new aches and pains, high blood pressure, dizziness, chills, diarrhea, fatigue, profuse sweating, diabetes, severe headaches, ulcers, joint and respiratory problems, lowered immune function, or increased numbers of surgeries and hospitalizations.

Social Consequences. Loss may disrupt our friendships, cause marital conflict, or lead to overdependence. Social isolation results when we withdraw from others or when they feel uncomfortable with our pain and withdraw from us.

Spiritual Symptoms. Unexpected and difficult losses may challenge our basic beliefs, upset our spiritual equilibrium, or shatter our long-held assumptions about love, life, death, and God. Loss may cause us to ask "Why?" and wonder if God really cares.

Symptoms of grief may remain acute for a year or more, then surface in waves and cycles far into the future. Symptoms usually diminish in frequency and intensity over time but can reoccur with intensity when some person, place, or event reminds us of a loss. Most experts today agree that grief does not occur in predictable stages one must go through to "get back to normal." Instead, modern theorists tend to regard grief as a personalized, unpredictable, yet transforming journey.

The Danger of Complicated Grief

All the symptoms described above occur normally in grief. Mismanagement, however, can lead to the severe symptoms associated with *complicated grief.* Individuals caught in complicated grief may become stuck in grief, unable to move forward with life.

Complicated grief may lead to serious psychiatric disorders including major depressive, generalized anxiety, post traumatic stress and panic disorders. Physical illness may also develop when the chronic stress of unresolved grief attacks weak places in our bodies or causes us to neglect good health habits.

For varying reasons, sometimes people grieve without the benefit of social support or other's recognition of their struggle. They experience *disenfranchised grief*, which increases the risk of experiencing complicated grief. Disenfranchised grief results when we deny or condemn our feelings or believe God doesn't care about our pain. It also occurs when others criticize our feelings or consider us too strong to need support, as happened to Shirley who quipped, "We're not supposed to have any needs of our own since we're in the ministry."

Social support helps the grieving process because it gives permission for painful emotions to exist. Support allows us to spend time in a transitional place, doing the work needed to move from our pre-loss state to the new beginnings we must make. Social support helps us face anguish, express pain, engage in healing rituals, ask for help, and live with the low energy noted by C. S. Lewis, who pined, "No one ever told me about the laziness of grief. . . . I loathe the slightest effort."[1]

Growth Opportunities in Grief

While it seems counterintuitive, Scripture tells us that suffering can work for our betterment (Romans 5:3). Since grief definitely qualifies as suffering, we need eyes to see that grief brings both pain and opportunities for growth.

An Attitude of Gratitude. We grieve because we love. Though loss hurts, grief does afford an opportunity to give thanks for the love we enjoyed, the love that remains in our lives, and future love we may find. Gratitude does not come easily in times of sorrow, but we can choose this mindset because Paul reminds us to always give thanks for all things (Ephesians 5:20).

Improved Social Skills and Psychological Health. The conditions created by loss may force us to learn new roles, skills, and competencies. This can help us achieve new levels of personal strength and confidence. In addition, grief may make us more realistic, patient, sensitive, autonomous, assertive, and open with others.

Strengthened Social Ties. Families made smaller by loss may grow closer. We may grow closer to friends by sharing our experience. We may develop increased sensitivity to and compassion for others who suffer because of our own experience with pain.

Spiritual Growth. Unexpected losses may challenge our beliefs and create mental, emotional, and spiritual upheaval. This upheaval can eventually lead us to an improved understanding of life, reordered priorities, and a broadened life perspective. Loss may serve as a catalyst for spiritual maturity.

Factors That Shape the Course of Grief

We grieve differently from one another and from ourselves over time. Each experience with grief assumes a unique form that we can understand only after the driving forces behind it become known. Those driving forces include personal, environmental, and historical factors.

Personal Factors. Personal characteristics influence the way we grieve. Examples include gender, age, health, thought processes, and faith.

• Gender. Men often mask their grief. They typically cope with conscious grief privately, downplay their feelings, intellectualize about loss, and focus on solving loss-related problems. Women attend more to feelings and more often share with others.

• Age. Living longer typically means losing more. Many kinds of losses naturally occur as we age, including loss of a spouse, parents, siblings, friends, employment, dreams, health—and often, proximity to adult children.

• Health. Good physical and emotional health supply needed strength for coping with grief. However, physical illness and some mental health conditions like anxiety, obsessions, low self-esteem, and difficulty dealing with emotions make grief harder to resolve.

• Thought processes. Loss can shatter assumptions and throw life stories off course. We choose how we will make sense of loss and what we will believe about life. Thought patterns and mental perspectives strongly affect the intensity of grief.

• Faith. Sound spiritual belief systems help us respond to loss with resiliency and hope. Biblical faith offers a positive way to make sense of suffering, and it creates trust that pain *will* eventually end.

Environmental Factors. Influences operating around us also shape grief. Examples include quality of relationship, social support, and cultural systems.

• Quality of relationship. Grief may occur in a more severe form when loss disrupts an emotionally close or a conflicted relationship. We may struggle more with grief if our lost relationship involved long-term, hands-on caregiving or provided some extension of our own identity or ego.

• Social support. As noted earlier, support from others improves our ability to cope with loss. Talking about pain with safe, caring others helps resolve grief.

• Cultural systems. Both social and family cultures shape the course of grief. Our culture's lack of patience with grief causes many of us to feel ashamed of our feelings and hide our grief. Family cultures also shape how we grieve. Upon becoming POMS, parents who place a high value on missions and individual independence may grieve less than parents who value group interdependence and care less about missions. As Suzanne put it, "My husband and I are not religious, so that adds extra stress to the stewpot of emotions."

Historical Factors. Grief is also shaped by the past. Both personal and cultural history affect the way we grieve.

- Personal history. Our pasts shape our response to present loss. Those of us who felt securely attached and loved as children may cope better with later losses. People whose personal history contains too many earlier losses may struggle more as new losses occur.

- Cultural history. We are born into history and shaped by the social norms that prevail during our formative years. Because American culture had a kinder attitude toward grief in the past, today's older Americans often talk more openly about grief and participate in more grieving rituals than their younger counterparts.

Understanding Martha's Grief

We can now draw on what we've learned about grief to understand Martha's experience as her daughter prepares to launch her career in missions. Martha feels a sense of loss connected with both her relationships and her identity.

Her greatest sense of relationship loss, of course, involves Angela. Martha knows she will lose her daughter's physical presence in her life in the future, and she recognizes a loss of emotional closeness now, evidenced by Angela leaving Martha completely in the dark while making such an important life decision. Martha expects the miles between them to prevent her from recovering personal closeness with Angela. She fears that over time Angela will invest more of herself with people living on the mission field and gradually cease caring about "the old folks at home." She even feels somewhat angry with Angela for choosing to move so far away.

Martha knows she must trade sharing life with Angela for only hearing about her daughter's life. Future contact will primarily come through e-mail and long-distance calls, which Martha believes are impersonal. Martha doubts she'll have the chance to mentor Angela in the future because her daughter will live in a culture Martha knows nothing about.

Perhaps worst of all, Martha expects Angela's decision means she will miss knowing any children born to her daughter on the mission field. At the moment, Martha can only imagine how bad that will feel.

Martha also expects to suffer losses in other relationships. She doubts she can continue to fit in with her friends, since all of them participate actively in the lives of their own families who live nearby. She worries that she and Ron might experience a full-blown marital crisis once they have no children to serve as a buffer between them and to help them avoid facing some festering marital problems.

Finally, Martha even fears her own life might become meaningless if she has no family to nurture. She identifies herself as a mom, hoping to soon make a smooth transition into the role of grandma. Now, with few marketable skills, Martha wonders what she will do with herself. Angela's move means Martha will have to surrender a significant part of her identity.

As Martha encounters relationship and identity losses, many factors will affect the course of her grief. These factors exist within and around her and influence her from the past.

Personal Factors Influencing Martha's Grief

Martha's femininity helped her acknowledge her feelings and finally share them with a friend. These choices will help her cope better with grief.

Besides Angela's move, Martha must simultaneously cope with other losses common to middle age. Within the last two years, her mother died, her two sons moved away, and she became mildly diabetic. She anticipates moving from her home of thirty years shortly after Ron retires in eight months. The burden of multiple losses related to her stage of life will make it harder for Martha to resolve her grief.

Martha's generally good physical health gives her strength to cope with stress. Her low self-esteem, however, will hinder her ability to grieve well because she does not accept her own feelings.

Martha's thought processes and ways of making meaning contribute to her distress. She erroneously believes that geographic distance necessarily rules out closeness with Angela and any future grandchildren. Her overdependence on the roles of mom and grandma make it hard for her to move forward as her last child leaves home.

Martha's strong personal faith can help her hold together through her time of crisis. Thoughts of God's love and faithfulness as well as visions of family togetherness in eternity can give her comfort and encouragement.

Environmental Factors Influencing Martha's Grief

The ambiguous and conflicted quality of Martha's present relationship with Angela increases the amount of pain she feels over their upcoming separation. Similarly, the tensions between her and Ron increase her anxiety about the future.

Martha's social environment contains elements that both help and hinder her efforts to cope with grief. Her close, supportive friends make coping easier, while critical members of her church—people who don't understand why she feels anything but happy about Angela's decision—disenfranchise her grief and slow its resolution. Ron's tendency to intellectualize his experience and to criticize her feelings does the same.

Historical Factors Influencing Martha's Grief

Martha lost her father when she was nine, but at the time, she did not grieve much because she wanted to protect her distraught mother. Now, Angela's plan to depart has tapped into Martha's reservoir of pent-up, unresolved grief and fear of further abandonment. Energy related to that old loss now helps fuel the fire of Martha's present grief. In addition, the more family-centered culture of the 1950s in which Martha grew up groomed her to expect that the generations of her family would always live close to one another.

How Martha Can Resolve Her Grief

Martha faces a dangerous opportunity as she grieves. She has an opportunity to grow as she works through her grief, but she can also experience complications or become stuck in pain if her grief is not well supported and effectively processed. The choices she makes now will determine how well her grief resolves. She could suffer serious complications if she continues to deny, hide, or invalidate her feelings. On the other hand, she will do well and even experience personal growth if she takes the following steps.

Recognize What Is Happening. Though no one has died, Martha feels the pain of loss. She cannot resolve her pain until she recognizes her grief. She needs to learn about the nature of grief and attend to her emotional experience. After recognizing her feelings, Martha will benefit if she puts her feelings into words as she talks to God and safe friends and writes about them in a journal. She could also benefit by expressing her feelings through outlets such as art or music, as modeled by King David (2 Samuel 6:5).

Accept the Experience. God created the natural process of grief. He sympathizes with our distress (Psalm 22:24). We should not condemn our feelings, which only frustrates the natural healing process. Martha will do best if she accepts her feelings, even when they seem frightening or confusing. She must not criticize her feelings or consider them a sign of weakness.

Understand the Causes. Martha will find her grief less frightening and confusing when she understands the forces driving it. After she understands how much of her pain results from her sometimes erroneous ways of thinking about Angela's move, her unresolved relationship problems, her identity issues, and her unresolved grief, she can begin to plan action steps that will help her move toward recovery.

Practice Self-Care. Grief takes time, energy, and space to resolve. Martha can help herself by slowing down and making time to experience and process her feelings. During this difficult time, she should avoid unnecessary responsibilities, postpone unnecessary life changes, and avoid taking on new tasks when possible. Though her energy wanes due to grief, Martha will do better if she makes the effort to get adequate sleep, exercise, eat a healthy diet, play, and see her doctor regularly.

Seek Help from God and Others. We naturally experience fear and angst in the face of change and uncertainty. God understands and wants us to find comfort and reassurance in Him and through the caring support of others. Martha will fare better in grief if she seeks help through her struggle from God and safe others. If praying and talking with trusted others does not provide sufficient support, she should talk with a pastor or counselor with expertise in the area of grief.

Actively Pursue Growth. In the best scenario, Martha will do more than just cope with her grief. She will seize the opportunity created by her personal crisis to introspect, consult, evaluate, and finally launch herself on a journey of personal growth. First, she can find ways to stay close to and enjoy family relationships with Angela and any future grandchildren. She can integrate her new identity as a POM into the rest of her life by taking an active interest in missions and by expanding her identity beyond her maternal role. She can invite Ron to work with her and perhaps see a marriage counselor to strengthen their weakened marriage. And she can ask a counselor to help her process all her grief, adjust her expectations, improve her self-esteem, and master the skills she needs to keep her relationships healthy in the future.

A Springboard toward Wholeness

Martha's story will end well if she accepts her experience and allows God to meet her in her pain and take her on a journey of personal growth. He is faithful to turn grief into a springboard toward wholeness and fulfillment.

I (Diane) can testify to this. I needed healing and growth in my life before I became a POM, but I had never been willing to admit that or do anything about it. The grief I felt as I anticipated our daughter's move is what finally brought me to a place where I simply had to get help. A wonderful Christian counselor helped me grieve my hurts and begin to grow as a person. The results have been immense: healed relationships, a better marriage, new capacity for friendship, and courage to trust God and make career changes. God has given me a great new life.

If your grief feels heavy, we encourage you to trust God in

your pain and look forward to what He will do. We encourage you to say with Nancy, a POM, "I am immersed in His hope . . . what a wonderful place to be! The black cloud is cried dry, at least for now. I'm leaving tomorrow to the Lord. . . . My letting-go process will continue."

WHAT'S MY ROLE?

Relating to Adult Children

Tears streamed down my face as I watched them driving down the street and out of our lives.

—a POM mom

Wayne and Brenda readily accepted an invitation to join a parents-of-missionaries group meeting at their church. Their only daughter, Annie, had recently departed for a mission field eight thousand miles away, and they welcomed the opportunity to meet with other parents who might understand the struggle they felt as they let Annie go to such a distant place.

After several monthly meetings, Wayne and Brenda found themselves bonding with the other parents in the group. A deep sense of trust developed among them, making it easier for all to look inside and share candidly their experiences and feelings. Before long, Wayne and Brenda began talking openly about the painful emotions they experienced when their daughter departed for the mission field and the discomfort they felt over the way the family had said good-bye. They recognized that some difficult family issues had gone unaddressed and that their connection to Annie felt fragile when she departed. Wayne and Brenda found the understanding, safety, and support they needed in the POM group to let their tears flow. Nobody in the group blew off their concerns or criticized how they felt.

Wayne, a doctor, had hoped Annie would choose medicine as her career, but Annie left home at age eighteen to attend Bible college, where she befriended Jesse, a foreign national who came to the United States to study. Jesse planned to return after graduation to minister in his native land. Wayne and Brenda thought highly of Annie's friend, who was capable, kindhearted, and obviously a true man of God. They enjoyed his occasional visits to their home and the opportunity they had to learn about his people and the customs of his homeland. But they were caught by surprise when Annie announced her intentions to marry him after their graduation and then to follow him back to his homeland. She intended to live the rest of her life there, eight thousand miles away from Wayne and Brenda.

Although they felt stunned by Annie's announcement, Wayne and Brenda wanted to support their daughter, so they threw themselves into making the necessary preparations for her rapidly approaching graduation, wedding, and move across the world. Despite their uncertainties about Annie's decisions, Wayne and Brenda decided not to throw cold water on the young couple's joy by bringing up their concerns. Everything happened so fast that there wasn't much time for talking anyway;

feelings and relationship issues were squelched in the interest of keeping the peace.

Wayne and Brenda performed beautifully. Annie's graduation, wedding, and move came off without a hitch. Other than everyone shedding tears at the airport and confessing they would miss one another, Annie and Jesse set off for their new life without enduring painful discussions, facing negative emotions, or being burdened by the needs of parents left behind. In the popular (but not biblical!) sense, Wayne and Brenda conducted themselves as saints.

Until they began meeting with other POMs, Wayne and Brenda struggled in private with their emotional pain and concerns about Annie, without validation or support from anyone else. They felt confused by the strain in their relationship with their daughter. They wondered if they'd done something wrong, and they wondered what their role was now that she lived so far away.

A Relational Perfect Storm

Before I (Cheryl) tell you more of Wayne and Brenda's story, let's pause to focus on the pain these POMs felt as their young-adult daughter left for the mission field. Their pain reflects that experienced by many of the POMs we meet.

A Natural Process . . .

Because of all the ramifications associated with extreme geographical separation, POMs naturally hurt when a child departs for the mission field. But their pain increases exponentially when their child leaves for the mission field at a time when the parent/adult-child relationship feels strained and unsettled, which often happens! Such strain can stem from parenting mistakes or the insensitive actions of the adult child. Many times, however, strain results simply because the relationship between parents and children has started to change.

Parent/child relationships necessarily change when a young adult leaves the nest. Both parents and offspring can feel awkward and uncertain about how to relate to each other during this time of transition. Relationships previously grounded on the rock-solid foundation of parental authority become challenged when adult children start to claim their own authority. Relationships that once felt stable begin to feel unstable, as if built on shifting sand. Members of both generations may wonder what their relationship will look like in the future and grapple with how to fulfill roles in the present. One POM asked, "How do I balance completely loving my children and letting them go?"

. . . With Added Stress

Wayne and Brenda experienced the usual strain that parents feel when their relationship with Annie entered this natural time of transition. However, their task of working through the transition to reach a comfortable point in their relationship with their daughter became harder when Annie decided to become a missionary. She moved eight thousand miles from home at a time when her relationship with Wayne and Brenda already felt awkward, unsettled, and undefined. Annie's move caused the family to endure more than the normal amount of stress that comes with the separation process. Wayne and Brenda had to deal with the typical consequences of parenting mistakes, Annie's youthful insensitivity, normal separation anxieties, and extreme geographical separation—all at the same time!

Many POMs get caught in something of a perfect storm when the stress that naturally emanates from a changing relationship with an adult child merges with stress created by the unnatural, long-term, long-distance, cross-cultural separation from their missionary. Caught in the stress of a changing relationship, Theresa wrote, "She'd rather spend time with friends than with us, and that hurts. We expect the miles will simply only add to the problem."

POMs often feel confused by the changes that take place in their relationship with young adult children. We hope the following discussion of the natural separation and reconnection process will make some of these changes easier to understand.

The Task of Separation

Separating from parents constitutes the primary developmental task of late adolescence and young adulthood. Young people benefit from moving beyond the perspectives and experiences offered by their parents to exploring the broader world for themselves. They need to develop identities of their own and choose for themselves how to make sense of life. Separation does not signal the presence of a problem; it signals healthy movement toward full adulthood.

The separating behaviors of our young adult children resemble in some ways the separation efforts they made as toddlers during the "terrible twos." The titanic battle of the wills that went on during that unforgettable time felt bad but achieved good. Every time our toddlers successfully defied our parental will, they grew in their ability to experience themselves as literally separate human beings.

The same healthy push toward maturity continues when children become young adults. They naturally want to establish their own social, emotional, psychological, professional, and spiritual identities and become more than extensions of their parents. In fact, we can tell we've started viewing our children as adults when we see their accomplishments as something more than a reflection of our parenting ability.

Parents can regard the separation efforts made by their young adult children as a good thing. These efforts tell us our children feel secure in their relationship with us. Anxiously attached young adults often resist separating from parents and often fail to establish their own identities.

The Pain of Separating

Most parents experience some pain when adult children separate physically and emotionally. While our adult children may feel joyful about their opportunity to set out on new and exciting adventures, we parents may feel left behind and a little sad when pressed to surrender the parental roles that often have become central to our identities over time. We usually invest more in the parent/child relationship than our offspring do. We feel a primordial connection to them and want the parent/child relationship to continue through life.

We may feel hurt and pushed away by the steps our children take to separate and confused when they resist or resent our attempts to extend parental influence or force emotional closeness. They want freedom to make their own choices (and mistakes). We should remember that our offspring's drive to discover their own uniqueness comes from God, even when their actions feel hurtful. They may make decisions that disappoint or surprise us. We may have to tolerate the frustration of knowing we could help them—if they would let us!

Parents sometimes become anxious about the future of their connection with separating offspring. The natural loss of emotional closeness that occurs during this phase can cause us to fear our relationship has a fundamental flaw, that our child does not love or appreciate us, or that we have failed as parents or done something to drive our child away.

During painful times of transition, mistakes and misunderstandings may abound on the part of both generations. Parents may try to continue in authoritative roles or force unwanted emotional closeness, fearing that present distancing will become permanent. Young adults without perspective may respond to confused, frightened parents in immature and insensitive ways as they try to gain space for themselves.

Other life stressors sometimes exacerbate the existing strain of an evolving parent/adult-child relationship. Common complicating factors include sibling rivalry, menopause, midlife crises, illness, death or divorce, and poor communication or problem-solving skills. An *uncommon* complicating factor involves the extreme geographic distance separating all POMs from their adult children.

The Joy of Reconnecting

Happily, the strain that occurs between parents and individuating adult children often proves transitory. While God intends for young people to give up clinging to parents when they reach maturity (Genesis 2:24), His plan for the family does not stop at the point of separation and individuation. He wants the relationship to change, not end.

Accordingly, the parent/adult-child relationship in healthy families typically improves once offspring feel sufficiently separated. Although we as parents often remain more invested in the relationship, our adult children will always care deeply about us, even when our relationships are conflicted and broken. Adult children deeply desire connection with their parents and have an irradicable need for parental approval and overarching blessing.

Scripture contains many examples of parent/adult-child relationships that lasted a lifetime. Perhaps the most poignant example comes from the life of Jesus, who maintained connection with and showed concern for His own mother until the day He died (John 19:26). While on the greatest mission of all time, Jesus stayed connected to His mother, Mary.

If we manage to respect our adult children's need to separate from us during early adulthood, if we support their developmental work and manage reasonable self-control through stormy transitional times, our adult children will likely complete their separation work, establish their independent identities, and return to us in search of a close, personal relationship by the time they reach thirty. However, something will have changed because of the separating process: when they return, they will not come back to be our children; they will return as adult friends.

The Problem for POMs

Let's look at the time it normally takes to complete the separating-and-returning cycle—usually a decade! Society's practice of conferring adult status on young people when they reach eighteen or twenty-one confuses things, because young adults in their twenties usually have a substantial amount of developmental work left to do after passing these landmark birthdays. Most young people in their early twenties have not fully separated from their parents or fully defined themselves.

The problem for many POMs is the extreme geographic and cultural distance between themselves and their missionary *while the natural cycle of separation and reconnection remains incomplete.* On top of this, if the missionary plans a lifetime of mission work, the distance has no known endpoint.

You may find your communication with your missionary strained, and you may feel uncertain about how to approach and relate to your young adult child who lives or soon will live so far away. You may wonder how you will ever reconnect with this child you love so much and fear that you never will.

Let's pick up the rest of Wayne and Brenda's story. Wayne and Brenda benefited enormously from their opportunity to share openly in the safe environment of their POM group. The work they did to look deep inside themselves and share their experience with others helped them gain self-understanding and can help you as well.

What Wayne and Brenda Were Feeling

Both Wayne and Brenda were sorry to see their daughter move so far away. They each had their own set of worries about Annie's move.

Wayne's Experience

Wayne found it hard to let Annie go because he worried about her safety and well-being. He thought her fair coloring might make her a prime target for kidnappers as she moved about in a land of dark-skinned people. He worried about her ability to maintain good health in a land of unsanitary conditions, and he feared she and her husband would end up in poverty if church giving proved unreliable.

Personally, he felt guilt over spending too much time at work and not taking more time to nurture a closer relationship with Annie as she grew up. He worried he could never make it up to her now, since he feared his health might prevent him from traveling often to the field.

Wayne recognized Annie had left without receiving his full blessing on her marriage and career choice. Finally, he worried about preceding Brenda in death and leaving her to cope with the strains of widowhood without Annie's help.

Brenda's Experience

Brenda had a different set of concerns about her relationship with Annie. She felt rejected and somewhat angry because Annie kept her out of the loop while formulating her career and marriage plans; she didn't understand why Annie hadn't asked for her feelings and opinions in the process.

Brenda feared she'd done something wrong because she had enjoyed wonderful emotional closeness with Annie when Annie was younger, and she guessed her emotional volatility during the throes of menopause had driven Annie away. She felt emotionally distant from Annie on departure day and expected the miles between them to keep her and Annie from ever regaining their closeness. And Brenda thought Annie would need her help as she got ready to start a family—help Brenda did not think she could provide from so far away.

What Wayne and Brenda Decided to Do

Wayne and Brenda felt bad about the strain in their relationship with Annie and began to look for ways to improve their situation. Inspired after talking with other POMs and a counselor, they identified a dozen steps that would help solidify their relationship with Annie, even across the miles.

Understand the Separation Process and Resist Fear

Wayne and Brenda began to think of Annie's separating behaviors in a positive way and to accept that adult individuation takes years to complete. Instead of viewing Annie's move as abandonment and rejection, they trusted their strong family ties would hold firm and eventually bring them into a healthy adult friendship with Annie. They made periodic overtures to let Annie know of their love and their desire for a closer relationship with her.

Surrender Parental Authority

Wayne and Brenda had already refrained from trying to change Annie's mind when she planned to marry Jesse and move to a mission field. Now they chose to continue their hands-off stance, minimizing the chance of conflict that could lead to further or more permanent emotional distance.

Speak the Truth but Don't Criticize

Annie didn't recognize, as she was leaving for her new life, that her parents felt left out of her decisions and feared for her safety and well-being on the field. Wayne and Brenda realized they had contributed to the emotional distance they felt with Annie by trying to protect her from the truth. They began to more openly communicate their thoughts, feelings, and needs to Annie in a noncritical way. Helping Annie understand how her actions impacted them would enable her to take better care of the relationship from her end.

Make Peace

Wayne and Brenda came to understand their relationship with Annie would not enjoy health until they acknowledged and resolved the problems that lingered between them. Wayne got the ball rolling by confessing and asking forgiveness for working too many hours in the past and for pressuring Annie to choose a medical career. He explicitly expressed his blessing on her marriage and chosen career. Brenda apologized for the moodiness she'd exhibited in recent years that strained their mother/daughter relationship. Both realized that admitting personal failures and correcting mistakes were the right things to do and would increase the chances of their family enjoying a close relationship in the future.

Devote Time and Resources to Relationship Building

Wayne and Brenda learned that relationships require intentional nurture. Adult children often become weighed down with family and career responsibilities and have less free time than their more established parents. Since Wayne and Brenda had more time and money than Annie, they took it upon themselves to take active steps toward building connection with Annie. They made regularly scheduled phone calls and e-mailed frequently, sent packages, took an interest in Annie's work, and visited her and Jesse on the field.

Behave as Friends

A counselor helped Wayne and Brenda understand that the interdependent nature of healthy relationships includes a reciprocal exchange of care, resources, and help. They learned that healthy friends recognize and admit their need for one another. They carefully discouraged Annie's dependence on them and avoided depending on her. This came hard for Brenda, who based too much of her identity on her role as Annie's mom. She worked toward developing a more rounded sense of herself, preventing overdependence on her part from driving Annie away.

In addition, Wayne and Brenda actively sought to build their friendship with Annie by remaining pleasant, respectful, and deliberately sharing power with her. They grew their friendship with their daughter by offering her emotional safety, acceptance, affirmation, listening ears, honesty, tolerance, and personal availability.

Celebrate Marriage

Wayne and Brenda began to look less to Annie for love and belonging and more toward each other. In addition, they tried to strengthen their bond with Annie by loving and accepting the man she loved most, her husband Jesse.

Seek Religious Congruence

Wayne and Brenda knew the faith they shared with Annie and Jesse represented a bond they could build on. They prayed for the young couple, e-mailed helpful articles, and took their own place in the world of missions by getting involved with a task force at their church.

Celebrate the Grandchildren

Annie and Jesse had no children when they left for the mission field, but they hoped to start a family in the future. Wayne and Brenda determined to further build their connection with Annie and Jesse by actively helping to nurture any children that might be born to the young couple later on.

Share the Family Story

Wayne descended from a long line of doctors and other medical professionals who took great risks to immigrate to the United States and carve out a family niche in the American landscape. Brenda came from rural folks with a long tradition of strong religious faith and service to others. Acting on advice from others in their POM group, Wayne and Brenda set out to help give Annie and her family a sense of belonging and continuity by sharing the family story, transmitting family values, and helping the family maintain cultural traditions.

Be as Healthy and Personally Responsible as Possible

As noted earlier, interdependent friendships do best. Parents who depend on adult children due to failing health or weakness can strain the parent/adult-child relationship. Wayne and Brenda took steps to protect their relationship with Annie by taking care of their own physical and emotional health, living as independently as possible, and trying to stay strong so they could participate in activities with the younger generations of their family.

Express Affection

Wayne and Brenda knew that despite loving Annie deeply, they had not done a good job of talking about their love. Previously, Wayne hesitated to express his affection to Annie because he felt inadequate as a father and feared she would not find his expressions credible, and Brenda refrained from expressing affection because Annie had hurt her feelings. Both Wayne and Brenda came to realize their reluctance to express affection had been self-defeating. They began intentionally letting Annie know of their love and affection, openly saying things like "I love you," "I miss you," "I care deeply about you," "I'm proud of you," and "I admire you."

The End of the Story

Happily, the pull of the parent/adult-child bond is so fundamentally strong that most parents and children work out their difficulties fairly well. As Wayne and Brenda took all the steps they planned, their relationship with Annie did improve. Both they and Annie wanted a loving, comfortable relationship despite the miles that separated them.

Still, the period of transition when adult children leave the nest can feel tortuous and present real danger. Mismanaged transitions and unresolved problems can leave relationships broken for extended periods of time and even permanently, subjecting everyone involved to agonizing emotional pain.

If you feel rejected by an adult child, please know you are not alone. One POM wrote, "Our daughter has obviously distanced

herself from us and has an arrogant attitude about it. It hurts!"
Another said, "I've been unable to resolve some issues with my
missionary daughter and her husband—though I have sincerely
tried more than once."

Parental choices are limited when an adult child becomes
rejecting. We can seek to change what we control, accept what
we can't control, and trust God to provide all the love we need
as we seek gratification in other areas of life. It can help to send
a rejecting child occasional short notes that communicate care,
goodwill, and personal availability for relationship.

We encourage POMs to work hard at building strong
bonds with their adult child on the mission field. Healthy
intergenerational relationships benefit every member of the
family and advance the work of God's kingdom. Large numbers
of potential mission recruits never make it to the mission field
because they do not receive a parental blessing. Some missionaries return prematurely from the field because of strained family
relationships. Parents, missionaries, and sending organizations
need to recognize the value of healthy parent/adult-child relationships and take active steps to help POMs and their missionary children maintain strong bonds across the miles.

DO I KNOW YOU?

The Challenge of the Empty-Nest Marriage

Now Bill and I are wondering what we'll do.

—a POM wife

If you have a faithful marriage partner, celebrate! One in five POMs that I (Cheryl) surveyed for my doctoral research had lost a spouse and entered the empty nest alone. If asked, single POMs would likely encourage their married counterparts to appreciate having a partner and to make the most of their present marriage. Cindy decided to do just that. She wrote, "Allan had a heart attack several years ago and that helped me realize we don't know how much time we have left together . . . but that we must cherish what we have."

A good empty-nest marriage can provide comfort and support to POMs who feel lost and lonely when their missionary departs. POMs whose other children move out of town sometimes end up with no family living nearby and have a special need to build a strong empty-nest marriage. One POM said, "We only have one child we can see even semi-regularly."

It's not easy to build a good empty-nest marriage. I used to believe the hardest stretch of life comes in our twenties, when we face monumental decisions about careers, marriage, where to live, and parenthood. I assumed that once these choices were made, the rest of life involved simply carrying out the plans made in our youth and later relaxing and enjoying the fruits of earlier labor. I now know that life usually doesn't work out the way we had planned. An old proverb says, "If you want to make God laugh, tell Him your plans!" God prefers to help direct our life journeys. He doesn't turn over complete control for very long.

Most of us have the opportunity to rethink our earlier life decisions when we arrive at the empty nest. We may feel ready for a change of work, location, or even community. "One thing that surprised me about the empty nest," said Marina, "was how instead of continuing in the church we'd chosen for its great youth programs, we're now looking for a church that has ministries in areas where we personally feel called to serve."

The empty-nest stage of married life opens up all kinds of new doors and opportunities. In fact, this life stage offers so many choices we can begin to feel confused about what to do. Consequently, before making choices, we should pause to take stock of ourselves and our marriages.

Taking Stock in the Empty Nest

Strong marriages happen only when partners know themselves well and openly share their inner worlds. The hectic years of child rearing can cause us to lose touch with each other and with ourselves. We must correct such detachment if we want to enjoy a meaningful empty-nest marriage. The extra quiet time many of us experience when children leave allows us to do some serious thinking about the state of our marriage and ourselves.

Taking Stock of Me

While some of us arrive at the empty nest with an excellent level of self-awareness, others have focused so much on child rearing and meeting external demands that they move into the empty nest without a strong sense of self.

Who Am I? Some POMs experience an identity crisis when an adult child leaves the nest and moves continents away. Shelba wrote, "It's hard when the main focus of a stay-at-home mom's life moves away—even harder when they move so far away!" Luellen said of her husband, "He's lost his sons. He has nobody to watch games or go out for coffee with. . . . It's hard on him."

Most of us hurt when we have to surrender the active parenting roles that have defined our identities in important ways. We sometimes experience serious emotional pain and feel uncertain about what we will do with ourselves in the future. Phyllis candidly shared, "My prayers turned from asking God to keep you safe and bless you . . . to please take my life away because surely I was not created to live with pain that . . . hurts more than childbirth. How can I live with it? How can I nurture when everyone is living so far away?"

In time, we usually adapt to our changing roles, but only after we manage to answer the following questions: Outside of my parent role, who am I? What do I feel passionate about? What do I find really important? What do I want to do with the rest of my life?

We can build great marriages if we first develop a strong sense of ourselves and bring that to our marriage relationships. Feedback from others can help us grow our sense of self. So can looking deep inside. Scripture encourages serious introspection: "Meditate in your heart upon your bed, and be still" (Psalm 4:4).

Who Do I Want to Be? After we develop a sense of personal identity, we might want to evaluate how well our identity fits with our present lifestyle. We may discover it's time to change some things about the way we live. We might want to become more assertive, less work focused, more sensitive, confident, playful, or giving. The empty nest presents a wonderful opportunity to improve self-awareness and chart new paths toward growth, even spiritual growth. Persons of faith take stock from a spiritual perspective as well.

Who Does God Want Me to Be? God has plans not only for the lives of young missionaries but also for each stay-behind parent (Jeremiah 29:11). The empty-nest years offer an abundance of opportunities for purposeful living. Some POMs get involved with foreign or local missions themselves; some begin to use long-buried talents for the glory of God and the benefit of others. We can find God's plan for our empty-nest years by searching His Word, praying, consulting with spiritually mature others, and listening to His still, small voice as He speaks to us from within.

Taking Stock of Us

Once we feel authentically connected to God and ourselves, we are ready to take the next step needed to build a strong empty-nest marriage—connecting in an authentic way with our partner. Many empty nesters discover they've allowed their emotional bond to weaken through the busy years gone by. As you enter the empty nest, we encourage you to assess the state of your union by asking the following questions.

Do I Know You? Twenty-two years as a marriage counselor have convinced me that many (if not most) couples do *not* experience emotional and spiritual intimacy. Problems such as busyness, multiple disappointments, self-centeredness, poor communication, and unresolved conflicts cause partners to gradually distance from one another over time. In some marriages, communication amounts to nothing more than an emotionally flat exchange of impersonal information.

Do I Want to Know You Better? As we transition into the empty-nest years, most of us have newly freed-up time and energy that we can channel either into extramarital relationships or into building a better marriage. We have choices about what to do with our marriages in the empty-nest years. Some couples choose to improve their relationship, some continue with the status quo, and others abandon their marriages altogether.

Many couples divorce when they arrive at the empty nest. External pressures that formerly held unhappy partners together begin to ease as children leave home and financial pressures lessen. In the absence of external pressures, couples must depend on their internal bond to hold them together. Too often that bond has grown too weak to do the job.

Happily, most POM couples we have talked with want to grow their present marriages. Nancy said, "My husband and I often struggle to understand one another's perspectives, but we have one quality in common . . . we persevere when the going gets tough!" Another wrote, "I pray that as a couple God will give us time alone, make us sensitive to one another, teach us how to pray for each other, and equip us to meet each other's needs."

We have a better chance of enjoying wedded bliss if we proactively decide what direction we want our marriages to take in the future. We must not sit back, just waiting for married life to unfold. Maybe you've heard the old saying that "when we aim at nothing, we will likely hit it with amazing accuracy." We can avoid this trap by taking time to answer two additional taking-stock questions.

Who Do We Want to Be as a Couple? Most of us get to choose how we will live our empty-nest years. In *How to Survive and Thrive in an Empty Nest*, Jeanette and Robert Lauer identify three roads empty-nest couples can travel. The first goes nowhere and leaves parents focused on loss. The second takes couples through grief and back to their routines; the third takes couples through grief and on to a new and exciting phase of life.[1] We determine which road we will travel by the life decisions we make in the empty nest.

First, we make decisions that shape the *external structure* of our empty-nest marriage. These include decisions about housing, retirement, leisure, service, and socializing. Some POMs downsize after children leave, while others add space so they can house their missionary family during furloughs and other adult children who visit from out of town. Some save their money for travel to the mission field or become involved in missions of their own. Some are active, and others are sedentary. Some remain on the go, while others live quietly.

Second, we make decisions that shape the *internal quality* of our marriage. We can choose to live in a marriage that feels troubled or mediocre, or we can take even a strong marriage for granted. On the other hand, we can choose active steps to build and enhance marital vitality. Vitality grows in our marriages when we know and share ourselves with each other, resolve problems that create emotional distance, and give our marriages priority in terms of time, energy, and money. As Cindy pointed out, "It's so easy for us to put our children before our spouses, and that is so contrary to God's plan."

Cindy's comment touches on not only our need to prioritize our mates but on one other important point as well. Couples entering the empty nest should ask one more question.

Who Does God Want Us to Be? God wants husbands and wives to be lovers. Marital love constitutes a central theme of Scripture. The biblical account of human history begins with the marriage of Adam and Eve (Genesis 2:18) and culminates in the wedding feast of the Lamb (Revelation 19:7). In between this beginning and end, God attributes the corruption of the human race to the breakdown of marriage (Genesis 6:4–5), provides examples of loving marriages in the Old Testament (Genesis 24:67; Ruth 4:13; 2 Samuel 12:24), and describes His relationship to Israel in terms of marriage (Hosea: 3:1). Later in Scripture, Jesus begins His ministry at a wedding feast (John 2:9–11) and becomes known as the bridegroom of the church (Ephesians 5:25). Both Jesus and Paul took time to teach about marriage (Matthew 19:5; Colossians 3:19). In light of the prominent place God gives marriage in the Bible, it seems clear we cannot please Him unless we give our own marriage a prominent place in our hearts and lives.

Taking Charge in the Empty Nest

Once we have taken stock, we can take charge. We can use what we learned during the assessment process to chart a course for the empty-nest phase of marriage. But first, please recognize that while having a great empty-nest marriage sounds wonderful, we must pay a price to have one. We only thrive in the empty-nest marriage when we willingly invest time, energy, and money, and we agree to make personal changes!

If this warning makes you feel hesitant to even try to build a successful empty-nest marriage, please do not feel dissuaded. God stands ready to help us succeed. Nancy wrote, "I was feeling sorry for myself after our family left for the mission field and not liking my empty nest at all. But I cried out to God for comfort, and He clearly told me my nest would never be empty because He was in it with me! Now Fred and I are doing better all the time . . . finally after forty-five years!"

God has already provided ample instruction in the Bible to help us know how to grow our marriages. The following steps for building a better marriage derive from biblical instruction.

Recognize Your Need for Love

God created Eve because He understood our human need for intimate connection (Genesis 2:18). Yet our culture encourages us to live independently. Culture even influences some Christians to rely on God alone and to devalue close, interpersonal relationships. This practice defies God's will as taught in the "one another" passages of Scripture and can even lead to physical illness.[2] God designed both marriage and the church to protect us from isolation and independence.

God uses the model of marriage to explain His love for Israel (Hosea 3:1) and Christ's love for the church (Revelation 19:7), because marriage holds a greater potential for intimacy than any other kind of human relationship. He created us to thrive on such intimacy, and He wants us to let go of our children in our empty-nest years and concentrate on growing close to our mate. Marina and Mark tried this and reported, "We have grown to love the time we have together."

Take Stock of the Present

The taking-stock questions given earlier in this chapter can help us evaluate our personal and marital situations in a general way. Many tools exist to help couples who want to take stock in a more specific way. A useful, more focused survey appears in David and Claudia Arp's book *The Second Half of Marriage*. Life Innovations publishes an elaborate, computer-scored marriage assessment survey for empty nesters called Enrich (see www. prepare-enrich.com), frequently available through church programs. Professional counselors have access to many assessment tools as well.

Whether you pause to take stock of your empty-nest marriage in a casual or formal way, we encourage you not to skip this important process. We can only build a better future marriage if we understand the strengths and growth areas of our present relationship.

Build a Vision for the Future

We need a positive vision for the future of our marriage in order to move forward. Marina said, "Mark and I dream big. . . . We'll probably never do half the things we think about, but the daydreams of possibilities are fun."

To dream, we must embrace the biblical virtues of faith, hope, and love (1 Corinthians 13:13). We must hope and have faith that making good choices and relying on God's help will enable us to overcome obstacles, resolve problems, and transform marital brokenness and mediocrity into wholeness and excellence.

In all likelihood, the fact that you are a POM suggests you succeeded beautifully at your mission of parenting. You raised a child secure enough to separate, generous enough to serve, and competent enough to merit financial support from other believers. Perhaps now you can lay down your well-completed parenting mission and adopt growing a great marriage as your next important life mission!

Marriage dreams need to support overarching values and goals. We should articulate marriage goals and values and then decide with our partner how to move toward those goals and live out our values in everyday life. Failing to discuss and agree on such fundamental matters will cause us to resemble confused partners in a three-legged sack race who pull against each other and fall down.

Practice Grace

Partners in long-term marriages know the good and bad about one another and usually have taken turns through the years hurting and disappointing each other. This happens because most of us marry as relatively proud and self-centered young people who do not yet know how to love well.

To fully enjoy marriage after our children leave home, we must forgive past hurts and accept what we cannot change about the present. God offers no other path to marital bliss. He wants our marriage experience to teach us about the value and joys of grace. Satan, on the other hand, wants us to remain focused on our pain.

God wants our long-term marriages to help us become His

godly children (Malachi 2:15). Marriage eventually teaches all of us who stay with the process that pride, selfishness, and grudges only lead to pain. As a result, we gradually grow more willing to humble ourselves and serve one another in love. This allows our relationship to grow sweeter as the years go by.

Most of us don't get to a sweet place in marriage without persevering through some dismal times. While perseverance makes sense in many situations, we do not encourage persevering through abuse. If you want help knowing where to draw a line in your relationship, we recommend reading *Boundaries in Marriage* by Dr. Henry Cloud and Dr. John Townsend.

Hone Skills

Communication and problem-solving skills predict marital success. If these skills were not modeled or taught at home during our growing-up years, we need to take time to systematically learn them. We can get help in this area from books, tapes, radio broadcasts, seminars, conferences, counseling, and mentors. Skills take time to learn and refine. Happily the empty-nest years usually afford the time needed.

Some POM couples with an empty nest find they need to grow their communication and problem-solving skills because having family on a mission field has strained their marriage. One POM remarked, "I can certainly understand why the divorce rate is so high for couples who have lost children. We've noticed that we grieve at different times and in different ways and this provides an avenue in which anger can really breed. . . . Sometimes I don't think he hurts enough." Another said prior to her missionary's departure, "My husband's frustration and emotions about several areas came out at me in anger, and that was very hard. When you think of it, I'd appreciate your prayers for our relationship in this time of transition." Still another shared, "Losing our family has exacerbated our adjustment to the empty nest greatly."

Remember How to Play

Playing together strengthens relationships. I came to fully appreciate this truth after meeting a young engaged couple who, after a long friendship, had fallen in love while swinging from a rope that carried them far out over a lake.

Play is good for our bodies, minds, souls, and relationships. We would do well to follow the example of that young couple and take time to play together. POMs who have started playing together find they like the results. Ellen said, "It rekindled our relationship when we planned a trip together to my favorite beach for just us. We also took ballroom dancing through our church and had lots of fun!" Cindy wrote, "We started walking together." Marina said she and her husband play backgammon together when he comes home for lunch each day. Laura explained, "I took up golf to have something to do with him . . . he goes shopping with me."

Given the extraordinary price tag of divorce, spending money on shared fun to strengthen a marriage seems like a good financial investment. Perhaps you should buy those recumbent bikes you've noticed or take that trip to the mission field!

Get Sexy

In his book *Sacred Sex,* Tim Alan Gardner emphasizes the spiritual dimension of marital sex and describes the experience as holy. "Every time we make love," he writes, "we are ushered into the presence of God."[3] The book explains how sex within the covenant of marriage provides an important opportunity to celebrate God's blessings, worship the Creator, and experience the kind of oneness with our mates that Christ has with us, His church. Gardner encourages husbands and wives to place more emphasis on the relational aspect of sex than on the physical activity.

God wants our sexual encounters in marriage to enrich our lives and give us joy. We can enhance the frequency and quality of these encounters by taking good care of our bodies, communicating openly, and doing whatever it takes to resolve any problems that cause us to shy away from sex, problems such as anger, guilt, poor body image, or low self-esteem.

Sex with our partners in the empty-nest years can be better than ever because we have more time and privacy to enjoy it. We can offer one another more acceptance and patience and share an emotional bond forged by years of facing life together. We should nurture this aspect of our relationship and approach it with a spirit of joy and thanksgiving for the life and love God has provided.

Seek God Together

God can use marriage to make us better lovers and more like Christ if we place Him at the center of our relationship. While we always need to spend time in solitary prayer and meditation, we can increase the level of intimacy in our marriage by reading the Bible and praying with our mate. Some couples seek God together by participating in a couple's Bible study or serving in the same ministry. Marina reported, "We've started doing prayer walks for our kids in the park near our home." Laura wrote, "We pray a lot together."

A Season to Reconnect

While it's not easy to let adult children and grandchildren go to faraway mission fields, married POMs have an opportunity to find comfort in the arms of one another. God has called your adult child to missions, but He has not forsaken you. He stands ready to help you and your mate launch an excellent adventure together (Psalm 63:7; Hebrews 13:6). He's done that already for Cindy, who shared, "This season of life has given us a chance to reconnect and enjoy each other again."

It takes a lot of work to build a strong empty-nest marriage, but doing the work is not as hard as living in a lonely and disappointing relationship. All kinds of help are available. Now that you have raised your family well, take time to enjoy your marriage. Whether your empty-nest marriage feels broken and in need of healing, sluggish and in need of revitalizing, or healthy and in need of continued nurture, we urge you to proactively work to make your marriage the best it can be.

Why not take the hand of your partner, stand face-to-face, and extend the invitation penned by Robert Browning? "Grow old along with me! The best is yet to be. . . .Youth shows but half."[4]

ALMOST MORE THAN I CAN TAKE

5

Coping with Complex Emotions

I probably need to speak to a counselor because I feel cut through to my soul.

—a POM mom

Most POMs find letting go of adult children hard under the best of circumstances, and many do not enjoy the best of circumstances when their adult children decide to become missionaries. Many POMs face both the challenges that accompany the POM experience and additional life stressors!

Consider the experience of this POM: "There are several other stress factors in our lives right now. We just moved and have no family or close friends nearby. My mother died a year ago, and my father's been in and out of the hospital since. We have little contact with our missionary son and grandchildren, who live in a dangerous place. I'm feeling isolated and struggle daily with both arthritis and the emotional consequences of my 'conditional love' upbringing."

The overwhelming majority of POMs that Diane and I (Cheryl) meet are strong people who have raised strong, adventuresome offspring. We also recognize that strength has limits! Like everyone else, POMs experience emotional distress when burdens pile up. Just as a sharp crack of thunder can send an avalanche of delicately balanced snow tumbling off a mountaintop, the addition of just one sharp stress into the life of an already-challenged POM can trigger an avalanche of strong emotions.

If this has happened to you, please do not feel afraid to admit your struggle and to do something proactive to address your feelings. The assertion that "I can do all things through Him who strengthens me" (Philippians 4:13) does not qualify as a rationale for running away from our feelings. We can only enjoy true victory in Christ after we tell the truth to God, others, and ourselves.

Telling the truth involves admitting that life often gets tough. My perceptive grandmother used to say, "Life's a job!" Sometimes stressors only drizzle into our lives, but at other times they rain and pour in! We don't know why God allows such oppression into our lives; we just know His children have never been strangers to affliction. Paul himself was "burdened excessively" to the point where he despaired of life (2 Corinthians 1:8). We can profit by studying Paul's experience and response. He survived his ordeals and finished well by doing two things:

admitting his pain and seeking help (2 Corinthians 1:9, 11, 16). Paul's approach worked for him then, and it will work for us today when we feel excessively burdened.

Complicating Life Stressors

Stressors that can complicate the lives of POMs laregely fall into one of three categories: existing personal struggles, additional losses, and anxiety about the well-being of their missionary.

Existing Personal Struggles

Perhaps you weren't feeling strong and resilient to begin with when you learned about your missionary's plans. You may have reacted to the news with strong emotions that your child and others found surprising and hard to understand. We think this happens a lot. One representative of a sending organization tells of the surprise two young recruits experienced after springing the big news on their parents: "They drove home to joyously inform their parents (who were in the ministry themselves) of their decision. As it turned out, there was 'no joy in Mudville'—their parents blew their collective stack!"

Negative emotional reactions sometimes occur simply in response to all the painful implications of a child's decision to become a missionary. Some strong reactions, however, have to do with those painful implications and additional, unrelated struggles going on in the parent's life.

History of Abandonment

All generations feel pain when a family separates, but parents may feel the most pain because they are the ones left behind. Abandonment hurts. We have a primal fear of abandonment from infancy on. The pain we suffer from parental absence or rejection, loss of a romantic partner or special friend, loss of a promotion, or social exclusion tends to accumulate over time. We may begin to blame ourselves, feel unlovable, and generally invalidate ourselves to ourselves if we suffer too much abandonment over time.

You may feel truly heartbroken when an adult child decides to move far away if you have suffered a great deal in the past due to abandonment. Kay said, "In my heart of hearts, I long for them to want me to be a part of their everyday lives." Your response may include abnormally intense grief, heightened fear of future abandonment, and greater distance from a sense of self-worth.

Overdependence on Role as Parent

We can only wonder how the TV characters June and Ward Cleaver would have responded to becoming POMs. The Cleavers were a tightly knit family!

June might have struggled fiercely, because she was focused almost entirely on her family. Today's women have more lifestyle options than their counterparts in the 1950s, although many women's lives continue to focus primarily on family. "I'd centered my life around them as a stay-at-home mom," said Nancy. You will likely grieve more as a POM mom if family has become your raison d'etre.

Ward Cleaver may have agonized less than June, but he would have missed the boys he'd devoted himself to for so long. Dads will likely have more trouble adjusting as POMs if they have counted on having their children follow them into the family business, profession, or ministry.

Social Isolation

Loneliness is a growing problem today for many reasons. Our culture seems to value achievement more than interpersonal closeness. People in leadership often do not want anyone to get close enough to see their weaknesses and vulnerabilities. Busyness and electronic media keep us from growing our relationships, as do churches with programs that facilitate nothing more personal than study and superficial fellowship.

You may have relied too much on family to meet your needs for personal closeness because you've been busy or never developed strong social skills. If so, your missionary's departure for the field will leave a particularly painful void in your life.

Troubled Marriage

As we discussed in the previous chapter, most couples come face-to-face with long-neglected marital problems when they begin spending more time alone in the empty nest. As POMs, you and your partner may find yourselves more alone and more dependent on each other for companionship than parents who have adult children and grandchildren living nearby. Consequently, you may suffer more intensely from any unresolved marital problems.

Personal Illness

Health problems often trigger grief because they bring about so many kinds of losses, including loss of independence, control, lifestyle, positive body image, personal identity, or social and professional roles. Relationships can be lost if family members or friends feel uncomfortable with illness and decide to distance themselves emotionally. Many illnesses bring into our lives pain, financial burdens, uncertainty, and change. The consequences of illness can trigger anger, fear, helplessness, hopelessness, resentment, damaged self-esteem, or depression.

We suffer more through illness when others fail to recognize our distress or offer support. Such neglect occurs most often with invisible or socially unsanctioned conditions such as autoimmune disorders, disfiguring conditions, and mental illness.

We cope better when we receive support from others during times of illness. Connie, our dear friend in Cincinnati who battled cancer while her missionary son served in eastern Europe, helped us see the positive difference support can make:

> I cry very easily . . . I *am* a crier. It has been hard without Mark. But he's really good; he calls me at least once a week, sometimes twice. My daughter calls every single night. My other son calls me every morning when he gets to work. . . . I have total support from my children. I've never felt they weren't there. I know I can get hold of Mark if I need him. I think I am more fortunate by him

being over there because I had people all over the world praying for me. I've never felt neglected.

Unresolved Grief over Past Losses

The longer we live, the more we lose. Actively grieving after a loss can help us grow. We live in a culture, however, that encourages us to stifle grief. When we do this, we frustrate a natural process and end up living with substantial amounts of unresolved emotional pain. New losses that occur may cause our level of emotional pain to exceed what we can contain. Our strong reaction to new loss may seem out of proportion to the loss because it is drawing emotional energy from both the pain caused by the current loss and the unresolved pain from past losses.

Additional Losses

As the parent of an adult child, you may be in late middle age or the senior years of life. We all need to recognize that as we age, we face an increased risk of suffering age-related losses. One POM said, "I am struggling . . . because I'm losing my entire family of origin, which is a lonely feeling, at the same time my kids are moving out of the country." You may face separation from your missionary as well as other age-related losses.

Death of a Spouse

Experts agree that losing our life partner causes more stress than almost any other life event. It usually triggers feelings of shock, anger, loneliness, fear, confusion, and depression. And, losing a partner burdens the surviving partner with untold numbers of forms to complete, details to manage, and decisions to make. Widowed persons often cry uncontrollably and despair of life. They miss the one who was most important to them and miss being the one most important to someone else. Veterans of this trauma claim that only those who have lost a spouse understand the pain.

POMs can encounter a greater-than-normal challenge in widowhood because they have to grieve both the loss of a spouse and separation from their missionary. You may have to live without the only person who misses your missionary in a way similar to you and who could provide compensatory, committed companionship. You may have to face an avalanche of life changes, business tasks, and emotional trauma without help from your missionary.

Divorce

Divorce also brings the death of a marriage. It exacts an enormous physical, emotional, financial, social, and spiritual toll. It causes painful feelings of grief, sadness, hurt, rejection, guilt, embarrassment, anger, and fear of the future. Divorce can undermine personal confidence and diminish the ability to trust. It also brings increased risk of accidents, illness, poverty, and loneliness.

If you are a divorced POM, you may suffer in much the same way as your widowed counterparts. You may grieve both the loss of your marriage and the absence of your missionary. Divorce can force you to grieve both the absence of your missionary child without the comforting presence of a spouse and the loss of a spouse without the comforting presence of your missionary.

Parental Illness and Death

Today's longer life spans mean most middle-aged adults will shoulder more responsibility for parent care than earlier generations. Since our present culture has encouraged most of us to adopt independent and busy lifestyles, many of us may find ourselves poorly prepared to provide care for our ailing elderly parents.

Whether we are prepared or not, our parents will need time, effort, and financial resources from us if they live long and grow frail. Aging parents often require help with shopping, finances, housekeeping, housing decisions, transportation, medical management, and personal and emotional needs.

If you are a POM burdened with other life responsibilities, you may have trouble finding time to personally care for your parents and finding money to hire trustworthy help. Phyllis wrote about the stress she felt when her mother's health began to fail: "My mom isn't doing well, mentally. She's been in and out of the hospital several times since my dad died. They were divorced, but people around her and we think something snapped inside her when he died. She's confused, distraught, nervous, and unable to take her meds and obsessed with little things. My sister-in-law (wife of my late brother) thinks it could be Alzheimer's. It might be strokes. Something's wrong and she knows it, which is even sadder."

The need to make frequent trips to help struggling out-of-town parents can present a serious burden as well. Chris said, "Traveling to help my mom is getting harder and may cost me my job."

A parent's death does not bring an end to stress; it opens the door to a whole new set of stressors. We naturally suffer profound grief when a parent dies. We may also need to assume responsibility for making funeral arrangements, planning memorials, and sorting through and disbursing our parent's possessions—a job that can be horrifically complex and emotionally draining. Simmering rivalries with siblings may surface as well, compounding our pain.

Loss of a Home

In America alone, more than 20 million people moved in 2006.[1] Susan Miller, in *After the Boxes Are Unpacked,* describes the trauma and loss women in particular experience because of moving, calling their stress a "closet illness."[2] Nancy showed her understanding of this issue when she said, "Right now, the difficulty of adjusting to being a POM is multiplied by our move and all it involves. . . . We've been here for seventeen years, and I'm struggling with leaving."

Death of a Sibling

As time goes on, you may suffer the loss of a sibling. This loss can be hard to grieve because most support goes toward the surviving spouse, parents, and children. It can hurt deeply, because losing a sibling means losing a relationship that has spanned a lifetime and because family gatherings change forever. In addition, you may inherit greater responsibility for aging parents and affected nieces and nephews when a brother or sister dies.

Loss of a Friend

Losing a good friend through death, geographical separation, or relationship failure can bring deep pain because it means the loss of love, trust, security, safety, companionship, and emotional support. It will also hurt to lose a friend who has helped you through your adjustment as a POM.

Loss of Employment

You may face losing your job due to retirement, downsizing, or health problems (personal or parental) near the time your missionary moves to the field. An end to your job can trigger strong, unexpected emotions, such as numbness, anxiety, depression, embarrassment, powerlessness, distrust, self-blame, paranoia, hostility, jealousy, self-consciousness, loss of confidence, and feelings of failure. Losing a job can also trigger grief when it causes a loss of needed money, lifestyle, identity, productivity, and community.

Loss of Another Child

Losing a child for any reason is a wrenching experience that naturally results in grief and sadness. Losing more than one child can be truly overwhelming for a parent.

You may find yourself separated not only from your missionary but also from your other adult children, if they move away because of work or to live near their spouse's family. Or you may become separated from another child because of unresolved conflicts. Some POMs even face the tragic death of another child.

Anxiety about Missionary Family Members

POMs often struggle with concerns for the safety and well-being of their missionary family. One said, "Horror stories about what happens to missionaries awaken me in the night." At least three kinds of circumstances trouble POMs.

Single Missionary

You may worry if your missionary, particularly a daughter, leaves for the field without the benefit of a spouse to provide protection, support, and care. One POM received a note from her son-in-law, a missionary in a remote part of Zaire, that said, "I hope you are not too upset with me dragging your daughter and grandchildren halfway around the world." She wrote back, "I don't think of it as you taking my daughter and grandchildren off to the ends of the earth. I think of it as God sending them there and then being loving enough to send a strong man like you along with them."

If your missionary is single, you may fear she will be lonely or a lonely workaholic. You may worry about her physical safety as you lie awake at night thinking about the physical dangers she could face alone. Donna and David didn't rest easily for a while after hearing that their daughter Lydia, on an internship in Africa, entered her room and shut the door before noticing a green mamba (one of the most dangerous snakes in Africa) hanging from the coat hook on the back of her door!

Dangerous Mission Field

If your child serves in a particularly dangerous place, you will surely experience more stress than the average POM. David, the POM just mentioned, reflected on the destination of his missionary daughter: "The environment itself is dangerous, and even as a Christian dad I struggle with entrusting my daughter to God's care in a place where there are 'lions and tigers and bears'—not to mention poisonous snakes, insects, and possible terrorists!" David's sister-in-law, also a missionary, said, "My mom was a bit apprehensive about our living conditions. . . . Once she saw photos of our place with the barred windows, she had a lot of misgivings."

You will, of course, feel anxious at times if your child serves in a place where political unrest poses a threat of violence. Your angst may seem "through the roof" if your missionary's work leaves him or her vulnerable to oppressive regimes that persecute, abuse, imprison, or even murder missionaries. You may become frightened by things you hear through the media without knowing if your missionary remains safe.

Troubled Missionary Marriage or Mental Health Problems

Though we tend to idealize missionaries, they fall victim to human foibles like the rest of us. Sending organizations try to screen for problems before missionaries leave for the field, but some problems simply slip through the screening process. You may feel particularly frustrated and helpless if your missionary child struggles with a difficult marriage while far from home. One POM mom wrote:

> Our son-in-law is a good man when he's walking in the Spirit, but when he steps out, he is controlling and does many things that are emotionally abusive. Sadly, our daughter allows it, misled by the whole authority thing. I worry because they are in a country where wife abuse is accepted and where there is no place for a woman in need of help to go. It's hard for me to write about this . . . but the truth about mental illness and abuse on the mission field needs to come out. It is not rare for missionary wives to become depressed.

Handling Complex Emotions

The stress you experience as a POM can combine with stresses from other life circumstances, generating a frightening emotional storm. However, we have no reason to fear even strong emotions; they will not harm us. We see in David's lamenting psalms, in the life of Christ, and in Paul's experience that pain, suffering, and strong emotions are a normal part of life. We mainly need to know how to cope when emotional storms arise, and God's Word offers much wisdom on this subject.

Be Still and Identify Your Feelings

It takes time and energy to manage complex emotions. Therefore, if you feel overwhelmed by strong feelings, make lifestyle adjustments that free up time and energy for you to address them. Until the emotional storm subsides, you may have to set stronger boundaries, postpone unnecessary projects, or delay unnecessary changes. If you stay too busy to address your feelings, you will neither resolve them nor move forward with life in a healthy way. Jesus understood this. As He carried the heaviest burden of all time, He frequently withdrew to lonely places (Luke 5:16).

During stressful times, we need to spend time alone the way Jesus did in order to face the full intensity of our emotions and discern their nature. We may discover we feel anger, fear, hurt, loneliness, self-loathing, hopelessness, or all of the above! We can tell God what we feel. It can help to write your feelings the way David did:

> I am poured out like water,
>> And all my bones are out of joint;
>> My heart is like wax;
>> It is melted within me.
> My strength is dried up like a potsherd.
>> *—Psalm 22:14–15*

Accept What You're Feeling

We need to get comfortable with our feelings and refuse to apologize for what we feel. We do not choose feelings; emotions have no morality of their own. Beware of well-meaning Christians who erroneously use the word *should* in connection with feelings.

Emotions represent an involuntary response to an experience. If I put my hand on a hot stove, it burns because of the way God made me. If you tell me it shouldn't, your judgmental response diminishes our relationship and encourages me to feel ashamed of my nature. Too many POMs feel ashamed of their feelings. "I feel like a whiner and complainer after typing up what I wrote in my journal," said one. "Maybe you can use it as a bad example of a missionary mom." Another said of her daughter, "I miss her more than ever before—and I feel really guilty about it." Feeling ashamed of our emotions only causes additional and needless distress.

We see in the Bible that David was not ashamed of his emotions. He expressed them in poetry that God chose to preserve forever! The apostle Paul unabashedly stated that he despaired of life. The hardships David and Paul faced were severe, making their feelings easy enough to understand. Similarly, the hardships POMs face make their feelings easy enough to understand as well.

God does not condemn our feelings. He cares about our pain. David knew this when he wrote, "[You have] put my tears in Your bottle" (Psalm 56:8). Scripture tells us that even God feels grief (Genesis 6:6) and that Jesus endured intense emotional pain (Luke 22:44). Forty percent of the Psalms amount to laments preserved by God to help all generations give voice to their pain.

Ask God for Help

Though the psalms of lament begin by expressing pain, they always move to asking God for help. In Psalm 22, David voices his pain without apology and then seeks help from God: "But You, O LORD, be not far off; O You my help, hasten to my assistance" (Psalm 22:19).

The New Testament also teaches us to ask God for help. Jesus "prayed more earnestly" in times of distress (Luke 22:44 NIV). Paul directs us to pray when confronted with hardship (Romans 12:12). God stands ready to help us (Hebrews 13:6); we must not fail to ask for His help (Matthew 7:7).

Ask Others for Help

Though our culture esteems independence and self-reliance, these practices amount to sin. In the Beatitudes, Jesus teaches that we begin to experience blessedness only when we become "poor in spirit" (Matthew 5:3), acknowledging our brokenness and need. The "one another" passages of the New Testament instruct us to participate in an interdependent community of believers where we can both give and receive care (John 13:34; Romans 14:13; 15:7; Galatians 5:13; 6:2; Ephesians 4:32; 1 Thessalonians 5:11). Paul freely admitted his need for others' help (2 Corinthians 1:11, 16). We need both God's love and the love of other people. Jesus cited loving God as the most important commandment but promptly went on to emphasize the importance of the second command—that we love one another (Mark 12:31). We exhibit pride and diminish life when we refuse to seek or accept needed help.

If you feel overwhelmed by intensely painful emotions, do not try to cope alone, or alone with self-help materials, or even alone with the help of God. We fare best when we have both God's help and the help of supportive people. Nancy, a POM, said, "I enjoy the quiet and flexibility to . . . have a good talk with a friend." Besides talking with safe friends and family, it can help to talk with a professional counselor who feels comfortable with strong emotions.

Practice Self-Care

Good physical health promotes good mental and emotional health. So in times of trouble, it becomes especially important that we eat well, rest, exercise, and keep a routine. We enjoy better mental health if we think on pure and lovely things (Philippians 4:8). That means choosing uplifting reading material and upbeat entertainment and avoiding programs and movies that showcase the seamy side of life.

Think Rationally

Although we should not judge feelings, we can benefit from critically evaluating the way we think. We do not choose feelings, but we *do* choose the thoughts that influence our feelings. That's why Paul encouraged us to change ourselves by changing how we think (Romans 12:2). Choosing to think on truth can help us experience peace (Philippians 4:8–9) and set us free (John 8:32).

In the psalms of lament, nearly every writer finds comfort thinking about the good nature of God and what He has done. "For he has not despised or disdained the suffering of the afflicted one; . . . but has listened to his cry for help" (Psalm 22:24 NIV).

Each of us must daily put on the belt of truth (Ephesians 6:14) because we have an enemy who lurks about looking for opportunities to fill our minds with lies (John 8:44) that intensify our emotional distress. He wants to sell us lies about God's faithfulness. Though we cannot avoid thinking the thoughts Satan plants in our minds, we can catch those lies as they occur, label them as lies, eject them, and intentionally think on things true and lovely. Doing this helped Nancy, who shared an experience that happened a few weeks before her daughter's family departed for the field: "The Lord helped me remember a simple poem He'd helped me write fourteen years ago when I felt overwhelmed. I needed its simple words to help me redirect my thinking. This poem helped me cope as my dear family left with our only grandchildren":

> When I live tomorrow's fears,
> I'm overwhelmed today in tears.
> But when my eyes fix on His face,
> I am immersed in hope and grace.
> —© 1994, Nancy Stoppelkamp

We can comfort ourselves during times of distress by thinking about and reading in the Bible of God's goodness, remembering what He has done, connecting with Him through prayer, and spending time with people who speak God's truth in a loving and compassionate way.

Expect Good Things from God

We naturally experience fear and anxiety when God moves us through uncertain times to His promised land for us. We can only achieve victory in Christ and grow our faith, however, if we remember to resist doubt as we pass through troubled times and continue to expect good things from God, who keeps His promises (Hebrews 6:18)!

God has a good plan for each of our lives (Jeremiah 29:11). He promises to reward in eternity our faith and perseverance (Hebrews 10:34–36) and to help us in present trouble by providing all our needs (Hebrews 4:16). We can expect good things from God, even during hard times.

Can you say with the prophet Isaiah, "I will wait for the LORD who is hiding His face. . . . I will even look eagerly for Him" (Isaiah 8:17)? I hope so. If it seems hard, please try. God stands ready to carry you through your emotional storm, bring you to a good place, and do good things beyond what you can presently imagine (Ephesians 3:20)!

It's not easy to be a POM under the best of circumstances. This road becomes especially hard to travel when you must cope with additional life stressors. Whether your journey is complicated by existing personal problems, additional losses, or concern for family on the field, we encourage you to accept your feelings, focus on managing them for now, and look forward to the good things God will do in your future.

HELLO, GOOD-BYE; HELLO, GOOD-BYE

POMs can meet the challenges of preparation, send-off, understanding life on the field, and reconnecting at furlough time.

SAYING GOOD-BYE WELL

Positive Preparations

Parents are the front-row senders.

—a POM mom

So it's decided—your son or daughter is going to be a missionary. Now the preparation period begins, which is sometimes called prefield preparation. This is a time for missionaries to receive training, find financial support, and get ready to transition from one culture to another. It's also a time for parents and missionaries to prepare their relationship to withstand the miles that will separate them.

Preparing to stay connected as we prepare to say good-bye is how we say good-bye well. It's a process that can start months, even years, before departure day. When departure day arrived, I (Diane) was much more ready to send my daughter overseas than I was when I first learned of her plans to go.

Learn about Plans and Preparation

One of the first things parents can do during prefield preparation is to learn about the missionary's plans and what this preparation time entails. Understanding plans and processes allows you to feel more a part of your child's new venture, especially if you've not done cross-cultural work yourself or don't know any missionaries personally. Feeling informed and included, in turn, helps you know more about what you're lending your support and giving your blessing to. Here's a look at what your missionary's prefield preparation might involve.

Deciding Where to Serve

Some of the first decisions to make are where to serve and how to get there. Your missionary may feel called to a particular country or area of the world or simply have interest in working cross-culturally. In either case, seeking out the place to serve and type of work to do may take some time. Mission fairs and conferences offer the opportunity to learn about possibilities. Talking with other missionaries, missions ministers, and sending organizations is another first step. Evaluating gifts, talents, and skills is another. Sometimes a summer internship helps missionaries determine the place and type of work that are a good fit for them.

Your missionary may sign directly with an established, independent ministry overseas, such as a children's home or a hospital. A second option is joining a mission agency and a team of missionaries already on the field or forming a new team the agency will send. (Sometimes missionaries are sent alone rather than as part of a team.) Mission agencies ususally focus on specific parts of the world or specific approaches to mission work, such as Bible translation or church planting. Another option for missionaries is to be sent by a local congregation with mission expertise. *Tentmaking* is yet another option—operating a business that provides ministry opportunities in the host country. Tentmaking is frequently utilized by missionaries in restricted-access countries (countries that allow in Christians only if they come with a defined, valued reason, such as medical work or teaching).

Deciding How Long to Stay

Generally, at least the first two years on the field are devoted to learning the language and learning the culture, two prerequisites for effective mission work. Not every missionary plans to be on the field for life, although many do. Some plan to go for five to ten years and choose sending organizations that support and encourage this strategy. Others go with the attitude that they will stay until God moves them elsewhere, anticipating that He could keep them on the field a very long time. This was the case with my daughter Sheila and her husband, Scoggins.

Evaluating Readiness to Go

Deciding to go is not necessarily synonymous with being ready to go. Most agencies and sending churches ask potential missionaries to fill out a formal application, which is usually followed by some sort of self-assessment or readiness-assessment tool. Cross-cultural work is a spiritual battle zone, and missionaries can easily become casualties if they are not emotionally healthy and strong.

At this point in the process, readiness refers to having spiritual, interpersonal, and cultural maturity, as well as experience doing ministry. Critical qualities for missionaries to possess include knowledge of God's Word and the ability to apply it, a solid prayer life, knowledge of spiritual warfare, willingness to allow the fruit of the Spirit to grow in one's life, willingness to sacrifice, the ability to interact profitably with others and to serve others, and cultural empathy and etiquette. Church leaders and other mature believers should be able to see these qualities in your missionary's life. They also should be able to prayerfully confirm a missionary's call to cross-cultural work.[1]

Readiness also refers to the personal character of the applicant, especially related to past problems with excessive spending, financial debt, alcohol and drug abuse, divorce, and pornography or other issues of sexual purity. Past problems in these areas do not necessarily disqualify someone from missionary work, but healing and freedom first need to be demonstrated over a reasonable time. Sometimes applicants are asked to delay or slow down their cross-cultural training and planning to address these personal life-issues.

As a parent, you may have valuable insight about your son or daughter's suitability or readiness for cross-cultural service. Offer to share your insight with your child, if he or she is open to hearing it. Keep in mind that you may still be adjusting to the reality of your child's decision to go, and if you're having a negative reaction fueled by your own emotions, you might not be able to offer objective input, at least not right now.

Decide where you are as a parent in relationship to your child: a college student not yet financially independent may desire or expect your input more than an older child who's married with a family or established in a career. Parents also need to be willing not to limit what God can do. I never anticipated my daughter living and serving overseas, but she took to it immediately with zest and grace.

Creating a Preparation Plan

After deciding where to serve and for how long, and after being accepted as a recruit by a mission agency or sending church, your missionary will develop a comprehensive preparation plan for getting to the field. Most agencies provide help with these areas of preparation, but the responsibility for accomplishing them belongs to the missionary. Preparation plans include all or most of the following kinds of work and training.

Personal Support and Accountability. We all need personal support and accountability. A shepherding group, comprised of people who know your missionary well, can be invaluable. Meeting regularly with this group (or having regular contact with these individuals if they don't live nearby) allows missionaries to have a sounding board where they can share honestly, ask for help, and receive feedback and prayer.

Spiritual Readiness and Maturity. Whether it's praying together as a couple, working through personal issues, or serving at home in the kind of work the missionary wants to do on the field, these activities develop the disciplines and fruit of the Spirit essential to serving cross-culturally.

Support Raising. Your missionary will develop a budget with help from his sending church or organization. Then he or she will need to raise enough financial support to cover the budget. Usually this means making presentations to churches and individuals until the needed amount has been pledged. "Most missionaries would say that the extensive network of prayer and financial support is a good thing," said Sue, a former missionary, "as long as it's not super spread out. It's not always easy to see that as a recruit, but God uses support raising in great ways." Sometimes missionaries are fully supported by one sending church.

Cross-Cultural Experience. Living or working in another culture is the best test of one's ability to do so. If the missionary lacks this experience, making one or more shorter mission trips before making a long-term commitment can be beneficial.

Preparation for Children's Care. Missionary families with children may need to explore options for child care on the field as well as educational options. Will children attend school in the host country? Or will they be homeschooled or taught by a teacher who joins the mission team for that purpose? Boarding schools for children of missionaries still exist in some places, although this option has received much scrutiny and has fallen out of favor with many.

Medical, Legal, and Financial Tasks. It's wise for missionaries to get comprehensive medical checkups before their departure. They also need to arrange for international health insurance and perhaps an international driver's license. They will want to prepare wills and power of attorney documents to leave with loved ones at home. They may need to prepare the paperwork needed to receive a visa from the host country. A forwarding agent, someone who handles the missionary's finances and legal obligations at home, needs to be selected and added as a signatory to bank accounts.

Relationship with the Sending Organization. Sending a missionary to the field is a partnership. Most agencies require recruits to attend special programs designed to acquaint them with the policies and procedures of the agency and the training and other kinds of help the agency offers.

Specialized Training. Some missionaries, such as those who will do Bible translation, need advanced education degrees. All benefit from courses that teach the skills needed to learn a foreign language, develop cultural sensitivity, hone interpersonal and conflict-resolution skills, speak in public, and raise support. Many mission agencies offer this training to their recruits or utilize the services of other organizations to provide it.

We hope that, from the outset, your missionary will keep you informed about his or her plans and preparation. If not, consider using this chapter as a jumping-off point for questions to ask your missionary either in person or by phone or e-mail. Carefully phrase your questions to be nonthreatening to young adults who are still working out what it means to live independent of their parents. "I'd like to understand the support raising process," for example, is much better phrasing than "Why on earth would you want to go through all of that?"

Discover What You Need

You may not have been surprised by your child's decision; maybe you even anticipated it and encouraged it when your child was young. Or you might never have guessed the path your child is now taking. Either way, the preparation you need is still the same. Take time now, while departure is still months away, to discover what will help you most during prefield preparation and make a plan to get your needs met.

Come to Terms with the Decision

It's interesting that the way parents learn about their missionary's plans often impacts their reaction. As Cheryl's research showed, parents who know about their child's plans early in the process are often more supportive and cope more easily than parents for whom the decision and departure are a big surprise. But there simply is no one-size-fits-all reaction. As earlier chapters have explored, it's normal for gratitude and trust to mix with fear and sadness. Nancy wrote, "When I first heard the news that our daughter and her husband and all four of our grandchildren were heading for another continent to be missionaries, the news took my breath away—not in joy, but in panic and sorrow. My only grandchildren!"

Sometimes God gives parents hints about their child's upcoming decision. I once received an e-mail from a member of a missions task force at my church. I was not part of the task force, never received any of the group's reports, and never received another e-mail from the group. This particular message, however, reported a finding that music was an important part of the culture in Bosnia and could be a useful tool for evangelism. My daughter is a singer. *Sheila could do that,* I thought. Months later, while I was on a business trip, Sheila called with the news that she and her husband were planning a summer missions internship in Bosnia. "Are you surprised?" she asked. I remembered the mysterious e-mail. "No," I told her, "I'm not!"

Other parents report that their child showed interest in missions while still in elementary school, and still others had teenagers for whom short-term mission trips grew into a passion for missions. I view these "hints" from God as proof that He cares about parents and understands how some of us struggle with becoming POMs. He cares, and He helps us prepare.

Remember that a good connection between you and your missionary is what will help you thrive as a POM. Especially in the early days of your missionary's preparation, consider how what you say and do now may either weaken or strengthen that connection, and act accordingly. One couple had this to say about their daughter's decision to serve with a ministry not affiliated with their faith background: "As Catholics, we gave our children what we felt was the best kind of education. We presented our faith to them the best way we could. So when our daughter decided to work with Campus Crusade, we were hurt because we thought she was going in a different direction. There were two ways to handle it: we could turn our backs on her and her new ideas, losing her and all she had to teach us, or we could open our hearts to a whole new experience and benefit from it. That's what we've done."[2]

As we try to make clear throughout this book, Cheryl and I believe that adjusting to POM life and thriving as POMs is a process. It takes time! The preparation period, however, is an important juncture. If you can decide now to support and bless your missionary's endeavor, whatever it takes, you then are free to begin finding ways to thrive.

Gather Information

If your son or daughter took a new job in a town nearby or one several states away, you would already have a good idea of what his or her life might be like. The shopping, schools, sports, churches, businesses, and neighborhoods probably wouldn't be much different from those where you live, even allowing for regional variations. Unless you've lived overseas yourself, however, you don't know what life is like in another country. Unless you've worked as a missionary or have friends who are missionaries, you don't know what missionary life is like. This can make even supportive parents uneasy.

One part of the antidote is information, lots and lots of information. We've already looked at the preparation process your missionary will go through before departure. You will also want to learn about the country where your missionary will work—what is it like religiously, culturally, politically? Who are the people there? What is their history? Is the country open to Christian missionaries, is it a restricted-access country, or is the country closed to missionaries and opposed to the gospel?

It's natural for parents to have fears about the well-being of their children and grandchildren while they live overseas. What kinds of precautions will your missionary take if his field of service is a closed or restricted-access country? What is the level of medical care, and what provisions are made for handling medical emergencies? What evacuation plans are in place in case of extreme political unrest or other danger?

Parents may also have questions about the missionary's work and his or her relationship with the sending organization. What does the missionary's budget include, and how is the budget determined? Where do the finances come from to support your missionary? What about planning for college tuition for your grandchildren or retirement funding for the missionary? How do taxes get filed? These are common questions parents ask, and you may have others.

You can take initiative and research the country your child is going to through online resources, newspapers, and books. For answers to other questions, you may need to ask the missionary, his sending church or agency, or both. Some sending organizations are beginning to provide information and answers for parents as part of preparing their missionaries. But if you are not offered this information, ask. "My mom loved listening in to conversations we had with other people about our plans," said Sue. "She felt she learned a lot that she didn't even know she should ask!"

The degree to which parents feel a need to have answers to their questions may depend on the age of their missionary, whether the missionary is a son or a daughter, and his or her marital status. But whatever your missionary's stage in life, asking questions is a meaningful way to show your interest, support, and blessing. One missionary wrote about her parents' questions:

> I am the first person ever to become a missionary in my family, so the subject is somewhat foreign to them. When my husband and I revealed our plans to our parents, their reactions ranged from supportive to semi-skeptical. What we have observed across the board is a general lack of questions about it. However, we know our parents have tons of questions running through their heads! Sometimes we feel we have to talk way too much when we are with them to describe our experiences that have brought us to this decision.
>
> Why should fear of talking about a subject keep us from openly discussing it? A little knowledge goes a long way and can soothe the soul. If you are a parent and you tell your child that you support his or her decision, then please begin to ask questions

about it. . . . Saying you support the decision and then not knowing how to talk about it can easily be fixed by asking simple questions. If your children are fearless enough to become missionaries, then they will be more than willing to show you everything they can to help you become a pillar in their support system. Parents, we need more of you—please ask questions!

Do the Work

I know. You already have a job. Maybe two or three, counting all the volunteering you may do. But I'm talking about something different. Your world *is* going to change, so how will you respond? How do you *want* to respond? What might keep you from responding as you'd like to?

Do you feel engulfed by grief? Does your relationship with your child need shoring up? Do you feel you must deal with being a POM all by yourself? Are there other life circumstances that make having your missionary far from you an especially difficult challenge? Are you technologically challenged, all thumbs at a computer? Are you worried that you won't know your own grandchildren and they won't know you? These are common problems that, left unaddressed, will negatively impact your connection with your missionary. Addressing them, however, greatly enhances your connection.

Let us encourage you to do the work of identifying issues, taking responsibility, committing to growth, and taking action to achieve it. Do you need to have a conversation with your child? Do you need to connect with other POMs or seek counseling for yourself? Do you need to learn to use a computer? Whatever work you need to do, use this prefield preparation time to do it. You won't be sorry.

Participate

Just as asking questions communicates your interest, support, and blessing, being present at important events also says you care. So if you can be there, be there! Many churches hold special events featuring the missionaries they are sending to the field. Mission conferences are good places to engage with your child's vision. POM groups and events allow you to learn from others who have walked this path longer than you.

One very important event is the commissioning service. If you are not asked how you would like to participate, speak up! Tell your missionary if you would like to pray aloud, speak as part of the service, or be acknowledged as the missionary's parent. In the hustle-bustle of planning the service, parents may be overlooked, and everyone can feel bad afterward. So speak up about how you do or don't want to participate.

Pray

Again, as in so many chapters of this book, we want to encourage you to faithfully pray. Pray about and throughout this time of prefield preparation. Michelle, a missionary recruit, said, "The fertile time of prefield preparation is so dense with experiences, emotions, and decision making. It is best that parents fervently pray for their children during this time; it is what we need most. Also know that . . . we may go through some trials while preparing for the field. This is God's way of maturing us for mission work. Parents can inquire of God in prayer about how to help their children grow and mature through these trials."

"I'm especially grateful that I can trust the Lord to comfort me, encourage me, and conform me further to His image even in this," said one POM as she anticipated the departure of her missionary's family to Sudan. "I've been praying for them on a daily basis, using a pray-for-your-missionary prayer guide I found online. I've been praying as they signed up with a sending agency, as they trained, and now I'm praying for our grandchild to be. Being a former Moms In Touch participant, my prayers have broadened as my kids have grown from birth to adulthood and now to the next generation. Here we grow further in our faith."

Saying Good-Bye Well

It's said that the word *love* is spelled T-I-M-E. Throughout the prefield period, if parents and their missionaries can plan to invest time together, you will be able to say good-bye well. Start now, even if departure is several years away.

Thanks to Judy Johnson, minister of missions at the church we attend, our family was able to say good-bye well. Judy's first piece of advice: spend time together. Part of Sheila and Scoggins' preparation plan included intentionally spending time with their families. During the year before their departure, despite college classes and jobs, Sheila and Scoggins made time for Friday-night dinners with us and Sheila's younger sister, and we also took a short vacation together. We made many memories. Our actions said, "You matter to me."

Judy's second piece of advice went to Cheryl, who led our church's counseling ministry: help the parents. Our congregation sent two young couples to the field within three weeks of each other, and both sets of parents were part of the congregation; a third POM couple in the church already had children and grandchildren on the field. Judy recognized our struggle. A ministry to parents of missionaries resulted.

(Thanks, Judy!)

"The prefield time is one of the most important times of a missionary's life," wrote Michelle, the recruit quoted earlier in this chapter. "It is the gestation before the birthing. Receiving all that we can from God and loved ones not only will help us on the field and empower our effectiveness, but it will also protect us while we are away serving the King."

ONE MORE HUG

Sane Send-Offs

Parents cry when their kids do great things.

—a POM dad[1]

This is the hardest chapter to write.

Saying good-bye can be wrenching, and as I (Diane) learned not long ago, it is even more so when there are grandchildren involved. But departure day can also be joyful. Often, it is both.

As support is raised, training is winding down, and a date is set for departure, the focus shifts. Now, the missionary is not preparing—getting ready to go—but getting ready to *leave*. We hope that spending time making memories and enjoying family activities has been built into the preparation period. You've identified any issues in your relationship with your missionary and done all you can to resolve them. You've participated in the commissioning service and attended farewell parties. The time you've invested has prepared you to enter the departure period and to say good-bye well.

Is this the first time you've sent your missionary off? You may be trying to anticipate what it will be like and how you might feel, but the experience is yet unknown—you're not sure what to expect. If you have young grandchildren, you may wonder how much they will change before you see them again and if they will remember you. Is your missionary returning to the field after furlough? You've done this before, and you know what to expect, but you might be thinking, *That's just the problem!*

The days leading up to departure can be difficult. For some, this time is more difficult to deal with than the actual send-off. Bonnie described her experience this way: "I think the time before Jon's departure was the most painful. There were times when I felt like my heart was being twisted inside my chest. I could physically feel the pain." Not all POMs view departure in the same way, of course, but many do experience intense emotions during this time. Nancy described her situation like this: "For about a year now, I've struggled with my daughter and family leaving. I have many resources with the Lord . . . but I'm still struggling! I've always looked forward to being a grandma. I know I should be excited and thankful that my daughter and her husband will leave for the mission field in August, but I'm having a hard time with my emotions!"

A good send-off takes preparation on everyone's part. Dave, a missionary whose family didn't want to discuss his career change, told this story:

At that time it was kind of a weird deal because we just started avoiding it altogether. Our attitude was "Well, let's just talk about the weather." But we all live ten minutes from one another. We started spending less time together, I think first of all to avoid dealing with what I call the eight-hundred-pound gorilla, and then secondly, I think, to start the detachment process.

Basically, when it came time to leave, I had my stuff packed, and we all got together and had a meal. My brother and I have a long history of playing jokes on each other, and the meeting was at his house. We had dinner and sat and visited awhile, and then I said, "Well, I've got to be going" and got up and walked out. Everybody thought I was going to come back and that it was a big joke, and I just went. And that was my way to avoid it. It wasn't anything they did; it wasn't their fault that I got in my car and started it and took off. It did make things a little awkward the first time I visited! Seriously, that's what can happen if you start the avoidance game, it can get to that point where you say, "You know what, I'm just not going to deal with this."[2]

In retrospect, Dave said, "That wasn't the right way to do it! Eventually, you *will* deal with it."

Departures also mean arrivals—your missionary will be arriving in another land, and people will be ministered to by the ones you're sending. God is sending workers into His harvest, and you're participating with Him! Remembering the benefits and blessings signified by departure day can sweeten the pain of saying good-bye. (The flip side is that it can also make you even more emotional than you might already be feeling!)

Prayerfully submit the situation to the Lord, and ask Him to help you and your missionary make departure-day plans that meet everyone's needs to the greatest possible extent. Ask Him to help you understand what your missionary is feeling during this time, what he or she needs and how you can help, how to use time well, how to handle your emotions, and how to think creatively and plan ahead.

How Departure Feels to Your Missionary

Every departure, whether or not it's the first, comes with inevitable stresses for your missionary. Missionaries know they must set their minds to be ready to depart. Until they actually leave, they have to turn their focus to the field while still staying engaged where they are. It's a fine line to walk, and they need our understanding and support.

Excited but Grieving

Generally, missionaries departing for the first time are eager to get to the field, and their sense of calling and adventure tends to override the sadness they feel about the family and friends they leave behind. "I just wanted to get there—to just be finished with all the preparation!" said Jen, a young missionary. Your missionary is focused on a checklist of last-minute things to do and is antici-pating getting through security and on board the plane.

Yet departing missionaries also experience grief. Dave and Annette wrote in their newsletter a month before departure: "Four weeks left! The date keeps getting closer, and we have both excitement and anxiety. An inner tension—a paradox. We are excited to go and know that is where we need to be, but at the same time we are feeling the approaching change and know that it will be hard. Fun, but hard. Exciting, but scary. It's sad to say good-bye to our family and friends."

Missionaries sometimes suppress their grief. Doug described his experience this way: "There is so much going on that you may not express your grief. I had unacknowledged grief all summer. I kept thinking, *This is the last time I get to do this.* On the plane I had four spells where I just bawled."

Missionaries returning to the field after a furlough have more experience with the adjustments required by cross-cultural life and service. They're aware of what departure is going to put everyone through. They know that getting back into life on the field, while they welcome it, might be tough. They may have more empathy for what family and parents experience when they leave because they have experienced missing you. They are often acutely aware that they are separating you and your grandchildren. Stevanie, a missionary, said, "Parents need to understand that we are already grieving the departure ourselves, dreading it probably, and most likely resenting the time that we have to spend getting things ready to go. If we are cranky, try to hear that as us beginning our way through the grief cycle yet again. We love you."

Busy and Stressed

Missionaries returning to the field after a furlough are also busy, and parents might feel shut out. Sherry, a missionary, said, "It is a very stressful time. Moving back and forth is time consuming and requires a lot of concentration. Missionaries are not trying to be insensitive or self-centered."

How Parents Can Help

Shortly before returning to the field, my son-in-law said, "Missionary life, furlough, departure—all are awkward, weird, not-the-norm situations, so it's like you're always living in not-the-norm, and that's just stressful for everybody." I thought *He's right; that's exactly how this feels—for all of us!* As a POM, I found that it helped me to temper my sadness at departure time by understanding what my daughter and son-in-law were experiencing and to focus on what I could do to be helpful to them.

As parents we like to feel needed, even if our children are grown. You won't know exactly what your missionary needs during the departure period unless you ask, but here's a roundup of possibilities.

Prayer

Let's keep this one at the top of the list. Your daily, specific prayers can lift up your missionary during this hectic, tiring time. Among other things, pray for sustained good health, the ability to get done what needs to be done, successful farewells with friends and family, safe travel, and a good adjustment at their destination. One missionary said about the prayers of parents, "It is wonderful to know that parents are praying for you when you are getting ready to go back."

Practical Assistance

If you live close by or can travel to your missionary's location for the days or weeks before departure, your assistance with any of these will be a welcome gift:

- Help pack, store, and ship belongings.
- Help clean as they move out of their home or apartment.
- Investigate a place for them to live after they have moved out. If there isn't room in your home, is there a nearby hotel?
- Run errands as time gets shorter and the to-do list hasn't been completed.
- Provide transportation if they've sold their vehicle.
- Care for their children to free them to take care of other tasks. "When the kids were small, it was great if my parents planned to do something special with them during our busy packing time," said Stevanie.

Assisting our missionary with departure preparations is good for POMs too. "Our daughter lived just thirty minutes away for the last year and a half, so I was able to help with the baby quite often," said Jane. "They usually stayed weekends with us, since we worshiped together at the same church; then they lived with us the last three weeks before departure. We were very much involved in their packing and moving, and we're storing what they wanted to keep. I cherish those weeks with them."

Making Good Use of Time

The details your missionary must deal with can be staggering, and time is a precious commodity as departure approaches. Often it seems there is not enough time to go around.

Stay Flexible

Married missionaries may have two (or more) sets of parents they want to spend time with before they leave, who often don't live in the same city, and they must allocate time for all. Keep an open mind and an open heart about how things must go, and graciously receive the time you are able to have with your missionary. Your flexibility will be appreciated.

The flip side of flexibility is being able to ask for time. "I'd really like to walk the baby down the street and see if the neighbors are outside," I told my daughter. "Can you take a break from packing and go with me?" She could, and she did.

If you are fortunate to live close to your missionary or can arrange to spend time in the city he or she will depart from, there is much that parents can do to be helpful. The best thing to do is ask and then dig in. Just being around can be a stabilizing factor, and often in snatches of time as you work together, good conversations happen, insight or information is exchanged, and memories are made. I remember spending running errands with my daughter and then stopping back at her extended-stay hotel suite one afternoon a day or two before her departure. I don't remember all we did that afternoon, but I do remember being impressed with Sheila's organization, composure, and spirit of adventure. And I do remember that we were together.

Good-Bye Gatherings

Another way to use time wisely before departure is to host a special gathering where the missionary can say good-bye to many people at one time. There may be many people your missionary wants to say good-bye to and many more who want to say good-bye to him or her. Yet it's impossible to spend one-on-one time time with everyone, exhausting to even try, and frustrating when it clearly isn't working. Sherry, a missionary, observed, "Sometimes life gets so hectic right at the end that you don't get to say adequate good-byes, and you feel a little hollow afterward." Try hosting a barbeque, an open house, or a reception where many can say good-bye at the event.

Good-bye gatherings can have a good spillover effect on POMs as well as being helpful to the missionary. In the months before my daughter and son-in-law's first departure, the church our family attends held several send-off events. In the beginning I was afraid my emotions would be on display, and I dreaded these events one by one. But I was always glad I didn't stay home.

Participating in events like these can be encouraging, even if it takes an act of your will to be courageous and attend! It's simply healing to connect with others and to realize how many people care about your children and grandchildren too—there will be people remembering them, writing them, praying for them. Events like these, attended with an open spirit, help us come to acceptance, and acceptance makes room for joy.

Time Alone

Some missionaries value time alone to help them prepare for departure. "It was helpful for my parents to allow me some time alone, to prepare physically and mentally for overseas service," said Jen. Some suggest it's best if one or two days before departure can be their own, with all the important farewells happening earlier. Others want to spend the bulk of their time just before departure with their families. "If we can finish our itineration and leave a month to just be with our families without pressure to travel and speak," said Stevanie, "it is wonderful." Still others want to spend time with their closest friends right up to the last minute.

Your missionary might want one last basketball game or cup of tea with a best friend. Expect and allow for this in the departure-day countdown, and don't take it personally.

Handling Emotions

No two people react exactly the same way, but still there's no doubt about it: emotions intensify as departure comes closer. You know your missionary needs support and encouragement as he or she prepares to depart, and you want to be upbeat. But if you're feeling sad about this send-off, you're probably wondering what to do with the emotions you're experiencing.

You might be surprised to find that you, your spouse, or your missionary seems somewhat withdrawn prior to departure. Sometimes either those leaving or those staying behind tend to distance themselves to make the actual parting easier. "We spend one to two weeks, maybe a month, disengaging before we come home on furlough, and again as we prepare to go back," said Doug, a missionary.

Or you may find yourselves trying to be together all the time, looking for ways to do or say all the things you haven't done or said yet. "I want to be with them every last minute," said Connie, a POM. "It seems like you try to crowd every last thing in. But there's so much you didn't get done, so many places you didn't go. You're aware of what you missed."

These days can be intense!

Tears

What to do about crying? Opinions vary.

"Oh, my goodness, I don't care," said Connie. "I'm a crier. I want my kids to know I'm there, and it doesn't matter what anybody else thinks. When Mark calls, sometimes if he says something very touching, I'll start to cry, and he knows that I cry, so it's OK. Even saying good-bye over the phone is sometimes difficult."

Other POMs who cry easily are not as willing to be seen as vulnerable. One missionary observed about his mom, "Talk of kids, vacation, future plans, how long before we see you again can make her cry instantly. We pretty much can't talk to her about anything. That was her request, and my dad's. I think it's not healthy, and she agrees."

Stories of people in the New Testament are not devoid of emotion or tears! When Paul said good-bye to the elders of the church at Ephesus, for example, the elders "wept as they embraced him and kissed him" (Acts 20:37 NIV). Certainly too much unhappy emotion from parents is disconcerting to missionaries, who most often struggle with their own grief issues, as we discussed earlier in this chapter. If your emotions are strong, however, sometime, somewhere, you have to grieve. Cry, pray, talk it out with a friend—maybe do all three! And please don't let your status as a church or missions leader keep you from acknowledging your true feelings, hiding them from others.

Around your missionary, balance is probably the key. "The time leading up to the airplane taking off is the most difficult," said Susan, a POM. "Allow tears and emotions to show, with some control, of course. They are God's natural way of grieving and need not be hidden from one another."

Laughter

While they understand and accept the role of tears as departure looms, many missionaries and POMs also value optimism and laughter as coping tools. My son-in-law explained, "I think what's really appreciated and helpful on the part of parents and family is the excitement of sending us back over. 'We believe in what you're doing'—it's nice to hear that."

Another missionary had this advice for POMs: "Be at peace.

Help me with routine things such as cooking, cleaning, and laundry. Be positive and upbeat. Tell a good joke."

Before Sheila and Scoggins returned to the field after their last furlough, my son-in-law volunteered to pray at our final dinner together before we headed for the airport. He gave thanks for all the good times we shared over the summer, and then he asked, "Please give us a festive time now." Ouch! None of us felt festive, not even him. But we were willing to try.

Think Creatively and Plan Ahead

Both for departure day itself and for the initial days that follow, thinking creatively and planning ahead are good rules for POMs.

Off to the Airport

Many families look for ways to take the pressure off the actual departure, to "keep it festive" as my son-in-law requested. The morning of their first departure, Sheila and Scoggins had breakfast at a local restaurant with our entire family, their shepherding group, and the church staff. Then we drove them to the airport, and their closest friends met us there. We made a Mexican restaurant near the airport our traditional "first-meal home" place, and sometimes we ate there before departure as well. Other times, at their suggestion, we dropped them off curbside at the airport and allowed them to wave good-bye to us as we drove away, which they said later helped them feel less like they were the ones leaving!

Laretta, a POM, shared about spending the day at Disneyland with her daughter and grandchildren, saying good-bye in the Disneyland parking lot, and someone from their church driving the departing family to the airport. Rhonda's family met in the church parking lot to say good-bye, and then her daughter, son-in-law, and granddaughter rode to the airport in the church van.

Lynn, a former missionary and a POM, shared that her family learned to schedule early-morning flights "so we could just wake up and go." Some missionaries like to say good-bye at home to friends and family, stay the night at a hotel close to the airport, and catch their flight alone in the morning.

One creative-thinking mom planned to go with her daughter to the field to help her get settled there! "Laurie has asked me to go along to help her get settled," she reported, "and I'm thrilled at the possibility! Lord willing, I plan to travel with her in the fall."

Keep in mind the needs of grandchildren as you think creatively. Mary, a POM and a grandmother, told how she did this after a yearlong furlough:

> I bought a charm bracelet for my nine-year-old granddaughter and secretly purchased a charm for it everywhere we visited together. When we went to the airport to tell them good-bye, I gave Julie her charm bracelet, and we went over each charm and remembered what we had done that year while they were home. She loved it. She is now fifteen and still enjoys remembering that furlough.

For our grandson Kevin, who was seven, I took a lot of pictures everywhere we went together. I made three collages of all the best photos, and a place in our town made them into three puzzles for me. I took apart each puzzle and put the pieces for each one in its own plastic bag. At the airport I gave Kevin the puzzles but didn't tell him what they were about. On the long flight back, he was very surprised to see himself and all we had done together in the puzzles. Our daughter said this really helped him to pass the time on that long trip. He is now thirteen, and once in a while he gets out those puzzles and loves looking at the pictures we took of that wonderful furlough.

Not all POMs want to go to the airport. Others can't imagine doing it any other way. "Openly discuss the upcoming airport scene, what each party wants or thinks they can handle," one missionary advised. "Also talk about the fact that reality may not meet the ideals." Parents who don't live near the city of departure and won't be at the airport must decide where and when to say good-bye.

If possible, suggested Connie, have a tentative date when you will see each other again. "It might be a visit to the field a year from now; but even at that, it is something to look forward to."

One last tip. If your final good-bye will take place in public, decide ahead of time whether there will be prayer. Many POMs find they can control their tears until someone starts to pray. If this is you, it's fine to ask that those who want to pray with your missionary do it at an earlier time.

What Happens Next?

After departure you may experience a variety of emotions as you adjust to the absence of your missionary, and as we've said before, not all POMs react the same way. "We've only this week said good-bye," wrote one, "and the roller coaster of emotions seems to have run out of control." But Bonnie, another POM, reported, "It was very painful to see our son go. However, I was surprised how once he was gone, I seemed to be able to accept it more."

Make a plan for yourself for the days and weeks following departure. Marina sent this advice to a friend: "Plan to do something for the day after . . . or the week after . . . or the month after, just to have things on the calendar to look forward to." She wrote that getting involved in ministry events can be a good distraction, and she reminded POMs that "you have a ministry and a life beyond giving birth to this amazing child."

You might want to write an e-mail to family, friends, and supporters, thanking them for their prayers, expressions of support, and financial gifts for your missionary. Journaling can be a great way to work out conflicting emotions as you adjust to your new role.

You'll undoubtedly be waiting to hear of your travelers' safe arrival. Plan ahead for this to the extent that you can, realizing that your missionary can't predict exactly how things will go. Do ask who might be meeting the family and what access they think they'll have to phone, e-mail, and the Internet in the first few days after arrival. Even a short phone call or e-mail will reassure you and bring some closure to the departure itself. "I am slowly beginning to adjust," wrote Nancy. "It has helped to hear from a missionary couple twice about the kids, but I long to hear their voices!" A father wrote, "I am doing much better now. God has seen fit to allow us a couple of phone calls and e-mails. Praise Him for Skype!—we can talk for free!"

Some agencies require or suggest restricting contact in the first weeks or months. "The plan was for us to have only limited contact with them for the first year," Marina said of her daughter and son-in-law. "There were reasons for this: for them to be encouraged to make relationships in the field and to help them acclimate to the area. It's a part of the 'submerging' process of a foreigner coming into a new environment. . . . We got occasional e-mails, weekly at most, that shared brief snips of their life, and this was good. I cherished every one of those photos, each e-mail."

Of course, pray for the needs of your missionary as he or she arrives on the field. The prayer guide at the back of the book may be helpful. "I'm learning to keep up the prayers, but keep them spread out," said Marina. "The immediate needs of my kids overseas are huge, but the needs of my other kids are just as huge in their lives. . . . And being a part of a prayer team for a mission agency is keeping me grounded in the needs of many, so I don't get overwhelmed at the thought of everything my kids need 'right now.'"

One Last Hug

When bags are packed and checked and everyone has hugged one final time, when you leave the airport parking garage to drive toward home, it can be reassuring to know that you and your missionary have done everything you could to say good-bye well and to experience a sane send-off. The work you have done will allow you to keep your connection strong, even as you both minister in different parts of the world.

"When I board the plane, I start thinking about where I am going and am thankful for the privilege of serving the Lord," shared Carolyn, a missionary. A dad wrote about his daughter: "We stand behind her as her greatest fans, wanting her to go with every assurance of our love and desire to support in any way we can. To God be the glory."

"My children are doing well, happy and beginning to build relationships with the people in their community," wrote another POM, also a father. "Although separation is difficult, I would be somewhat disappointed if they returned home without fulfilling their mission. I am realizing my own mission as a POM. It is important to the kingdom."

Nancy was sixty-eight when her daughter, son-in-law, and only grandchildren left for the field for the first time. Two weeks after their departure, Nancy sent me the following poem, which she had written when her daughter first experienced God's call to missions years earlier. "My struggle is still enormous," Nancy said, "but God continues to help me through it. These words speak to my heart again today."

May they speak to your heart as well!

So See, Lord? My Hands Are Still Open

Nobody said it is easy,
    opening our hands in release,
But Jesus said if we trust and obey,
    He will give us His peace.
I've struggled with holding too tightly,
    knowing that she can't remain,
And, in the process, I finally saw
    that I just increased the pain.

I've prayed for protection for so many years,
    and Lord, I don't plan to stop now.
I can't keep our daughter away from all harm,
    and now I've made you a new vow:
To give you our daughter again, like I have
    so many times before,
But this time for missions—wherever you want.
    I trust you to open the door.

So see, Lord? My hands are still open.
    Use us however you choose.
I'm trusting you for tomorrow,
    Knowing with you we can't lose.
Thank you for being my Savior and Lord,
    and making her your own design.
Keep using her as your witness, and Lord,
    keep loving that daughter of mine.
                    —© 1990, Nancy Stoppelkamp

DIFFERENT ISN'T ALWAYS WRONG

8

Understanding Missionary Life

*The mysterious Holy Spirit is on the move, and you
trust that He is using you.*

—*a missionary*

I (Diane) knew very little about missions or missionary life
when I became a POM. Our local church had been increasing
its missions focus for over a decade, but my involvement in what
God was doing around the world remained slim, limited to
financial giving.

When I realized my daughter was going to be a missionary, however, I discovered I had a lot to learn. From my own
experience as a POM and from the experiences of missionaries
themselves, I want to share what I have learned. The more we
understand what life is like for our missionaries, the better we
can sustain a long-distance relationship with them.

You may already know a lot about what's in this chapter.

Or you might be more like I was as a new POM. That's okay. If I can learn, so can you! Let this chapter be a starting place; by no means does it cover every aspect of missionary life. But pray about what you read here, and talk with your missionary. Put feet on your parental blessing as you allow your actions to be informed by understanding.

What Motivates Missionaries?

As parents seeking to understand and stay connected to our missionaries, learning what motivates missionaries is our starting place. The call, the opportunities, the need—these are what motivate missionaries to serve cross-culturally.

God's Call

Cross-cultural work begins when missionaries feel led by the Lord to go. Parents need to understand their child's calling, how it came, and how it impacts the missionary's commitment.

One missionary wrote that her husband's family asked on their first three furloughs "when we were going to get it out of our system and come home. It wasn't until they understood that this is where God had called us and we had no notion of quitting (unless He led us elsewhere) that they had peace with the idea of us staying on the field." It also helped, she added, "for them to know that we took seriously the admonition to honor our parents and that we would be there for them if they needed us."

Opportunities for the Gospel

When you consider missionary work, what images come to mind? Be sure your perceptions are not dated or unfounded. "It is an exciting time to be involved in Christian missions," wrote Patricia Magness in an article for *Christian Standard.*[1] "There is a sense of energy and urgency accompanied by creativity and joy." Magness serves on the board of two mission agencies. Her article details some of the creative ways missionaries are working around the world today, while acknowledging that "traditional church-planting missionaries, trained missiologists, and Bible scholars" will always be needed.

Missionaries serve by starting or operating businesses; by teaching English or Western literature classes in countries closed to the gospel; or by conducting "AIDS ministries, community health ministries, educational ministries, ministries to the hearing impaired around the world, and on and on the list goes," Magness wrote. Bible translation teams are welcomed into non-Christian countries because their skill at developing written languages preserves cultures that may otherwise disappear. International campus ministries reach college students with the gospel in postmodern, post-Christian cultures.

Support staff members are missionaries too, such as those who do administrative work for overseas ministries or those who regularly fly supplies to missionaries in remote areas. In all of these ways and more, Christians are finding ways to meet the needs of hurting people and create inroads for the gospel. It *is* indeed an exciting, creative time to be a missionary!

The Need

But the task and the need are still great. Ten thousand people groups,[2] nearly one-third of the world's population,[3] have never heard of Jesus. Sixty percent of the world's people are illiterate[4] and cannot read the Bible for themselves, even if it is available in their language. And in parts of the world where the gospel is known, secularism and postmodern thinking cloud the spiritual hunger of millions more.

Not in Kansas Anymore

Remember what Dorothy said to Toto when they found themselves in the Land of Oz? "I've got a feeling we're not in Kansas anymore." Wherever in the world your missionary serves or will serve, life is different from the way it's lived at home. The language is different, the currency is different, and the customs are different. How people view the world and make sense of their experience is different. If there are Christians in your missionary's host country, the worship traditions are different. This isn't Kansas for sure, and missionaries must learn and adjust.

Learning the Language

Language learning is often the missionary's first task upon entering his or her host culture. Sometimes missionaries take an intensive language course offered in the host country or elsewhere before they move to the field they will serve. Others find language teachers and tutors soon after arriving on the field.

Being able to communicate well is important not only for daily living but also for getting to know people at the heart level and for understanding their culture and worldview.

Learning the Culture

Learning how people live in the host country is also a priority. Sometimes missionaries live with a local family for a time as a way of diving into the culture and learning about it.

As exciting as arriving on the field can be, especially after long months or years of preparation, it's also stressful. Nancy thanked friends for their prayers for her daughter, son-in-law, and four young grandchildren after they moved to Costa Rica for language school: "Thank you for your prayers. [My daughter] is doing better emotionally with more sleep, after struggling to adjust to bars on the windows, daily rain, inadequate close playgrounds . . . no car, helping kids in their adjustment, and general culture changes. Their Spanish immersion is quite a challenge too."

The prayers of POMs and others can directly impact the missionary's early adjustment. Shortly after her daughter's family departed, Nancy wrote, "They sound like they are adjusting well and have met a family only a block from their home who are also missionaries with kids the same ages as theirs. I prayed a lot for where they would live for just that reason. . . . They realized that my closet is the same size as the bedroom for their boys in the first house they planned on, so they took this one instead. (So God can use closets for things other than prayer!)"

Battling Culture Shock

Along with language learning and settling into their new home, missionaries begin adjusting to the culture around them. Cultural differences go beyond the obvious—food, language, transportation, and housing—to include deeper differences: how people view the world, process ideas, and make judgments. Cultures clash in how they view time, status, cleanliness, privacy, convenience, independence, and what's polite and what's rude, for example.

Culture shock is real. At first what the missionary experiences feels new, exciting, and different. But after about six months, it may feel simply different. A few months after that, it may feel more difficult than different, and not just difficult, but wrong. The term *culture shock* refers to this feeling of being in a place where everything is different and nothing is right. Physical and emotional fatigue contribute to culture shock, because trying to figure out how to live in a new culture can be exhausting, confusing, embarrassing, and frustrating at times.

Here's what one missionary wrote about her family's early adjustment to their new culture: "The great days we called, and still do, I Love Asia days. Days when the prices are cheap, the revelations come easily, and the awe of where, how, and why we are here is written in every tropical vista. But there are I Hate Asia days too. Days when the heat threatens to evaporate you, the cultural environment is baffling, and you seriously question everything from your sanity to your very existence. And, of course, you feel so very alone."[5]

Good preparation for cross-cultural living can lessen culture shock but not eliminate it altogether. Usually at about the one-year mark, missionaries begin to resolve their culture shock and embrace the idea that different is not necessarily wrong. As they develop understanding of their host country's culture, they also learn to value and appreciate all that is good about it.

Unless POMs understand culture shock and the cycle of adjusting to a new environment, we can be upset by the difficulties our missionaries experience. But by understanding the adjustment roller coaster our missionaries must ride, we can be empathetic at both the high and the low points, while we also encourage our son or daughter to have realistic expectations and to persevere.

Experiencing Culture Stress

Culture stress is the result of attempting to adjust to and fit in with the new culture. Barbara, a missionary, wrote, "Many people have asked me about the big challenges I am facing. It's the small challenges like no water or power, lots of noise, tons of people that wear me down." Lynn, a POM and former missionary, said, "Just as Christians who long for heaven periodically feel like aliens in this world, people living in other cultures will periodically sense their own foreignness keenly and negatively."

Culture stress is different from culture shock but can be considered part of the adjustment process. Dr. Ronald L. Koteskey, member-care consultant for New Hope International Ministries, defines culture stress as "the adjustment stage in which people accept the new environment, adopting new ways of thinking and doing things so that they feel like they belong to the new culture. This takes years, and some missionaries never complete it."[6] Koteskey also says that missionaries who try to become an integral part of the national community in their host culture experience more culture stress than those whose primary relationships are with other missionaries.

As we've noted earlier, adapting to a new culture is hard, often stressful work. "Some people seem to believe that they can adapt to anything, even continual stress, without it hurting them," Koteskey says. "It just does not work that way." To decrease culture stress and make it manageable, he suggests strategies that include maintaining relationships in the passport culture, taking daily respites and regular vacations, getting regular physical exercise, and developing a friendship with a national family with no other purpose than having fun. POMs can be helpful by being aware of signs of stress in their missionaries and encouraging them to adopt the helpful strategies that can combat it.

Challenges of Missionary Life

In addition to adjustment challenges, living cross-culturally as a missionary brings additional life challenges.

Health and Security

In some areas of the world, tropical illnesses and parasites are a continual threat. In some places the medical infrastructure is very limited. Missionaries often keep a variety of medications available and try to have access, even by Internet, to medical personnel in their home country. When possible, teams in remote areas may include a nurse or someone with emergency medical training. Sending organizations develop procedures for missionaries to follow when a serious illness or injury occurs; developing or knowing how to implement an emergency-procedures plan is part of the missionary's training. Missionaries in political hot spots, restricted-access countries, and closed countries are coached in safety and security procedures—habits such as being cautious about giving out personal or work-related information, varying their daily route around town, and trying to keep open space around their vehicle in traffic at all times.

POMs' fear for their missionary's safety and well-being is normal, although safety can be relative, noted Lynn: "People forget that we have some very dangerous places here. Our four-year-old went by herself to the corner market in Tokyo, but we'd never allow that here in Cincinnati." Missionaries and POMs must find ways to live with their fears, usually finding prayer and courage to be the most potent antidotes.

One missionary wrote these words to his supporters: "We've been back in Cambodia for a month now, and what a rough month it has been—the hardest month we've had since moving here five years ago. Following two weeks of hitting the ground running while taking a one-two punch of reentry culture shock and jet lag, we got hit at last by dengue fever." In the same newsletter, he wrote, "Please don't neglect to regularly pray for missionaries around the world! It is easy to forget that we are at war with an enemy who hates Jesus and who uses multiple tactics to try to discourage and destroy us."

Some POMs may find themselves not wanting to know

about their missionary's difficulties with health and safety. But if we know, we can pray, and we reap the benefit of a closer connection with our missionary. "We shared everything. No secrets," said Stevani, a missionary, about sharing news of difficulties with her parents and in-laws. "We have this luxury because none of our parents are overly protective or anxious about things in general."

Spiritual Darkness

In some parts of the world today, the spiritual darkness is easy to see. "Bongkeab is known for its sorcery," the Cambodian missionary quoted earlier wrote to his supporters. "So much so that a Christian Khmer woman here . . . said she doesn't want to go there with us to evangelize. She doesn't want to be cursed." (He added, "Her concern is legitimate but ignores the truth that the Holy Spirit holds power over all other spirits.") In other places, the darkness is not easily detected, but it is just as real—cultures where the Christian faith once permeated now discount even the existence of God. Wherever they serve, missionaries feel the effects of the darkness as they come bringing the light.

Finances

With their sending church or agency, missionaries establish a budget and raise financial support to cover the budget each month. But financial crises can occur. Currency exchange rates in the host country may change, making it harder for the missionary's income to cover budgeted expenses. Unexpected financial needs may arise—appliances and cars break down, an illness incurs medical expenses, supporters may drop their support.

Another kind of financial challenge is deciding at what level of comfort and convenience to live. This is especially true in areas of great poverty. "A unique challenge for missionaries is choosing a standard of living that both corresponds to the local culture and maintains a level of 'creature comforts' that will keep them there for the long haul. . . . Where to draw the line, and who gets to decide? This difficult issue can produce enormous guilt."[7] One missionary said of her lifestyle decisions on the field, "It's easier to live with less if I don't feel guilty about what I [do] have."[8]

Family Life

Missionary families share the same concerns as families in their passport countries, but they must find answers and structure their lives within the context of a different culture. Where the family is serving greatly impacts how the details of life are worked out, of course. Riding a rocket train in western Europe is much different than getting around on a moped in Thailand.

Missionaries need time to devote to their spouses and children as well as to ministry. They need time off from ministry in order to relax and recharge. Finding the right balance can be tricky.

It may be that mothers with babies or young children have the most to wrestle with—how much time to devote to their family and how much to ministry. How should they cope with the isolation that young children, limited language skills, and perhaps cultural rules impose? Women need clarity and support from their spouse, teammates, and sending agency during this critical time. This is also true when women first become mothers and may want to transition from full-time ministry partner with their husband to full-time wife and mom. Many women find it possible to continue ministry through friendships with national women but struggle for a while with feelings of lost status.

As we noted in chapter 6, how to educate children in the family may be a concern. Missionary parents have to weigh all the options available and come to clarity about what is best for their children and their family at each stage of life. And as we will discuss later in this chapter, missionaries must be aware of the Third Culture Kid experience and do all they can to help their children develop a sense of connection to their passport culture even while living on the field. (*Third Culture Kids* are those who grow up not fully identifying with their parents' home culture or the culture of the country where they are raised.)

Team Relationships

In some ways living, working, and ministering as a cross-cultural Christian is not unlike living, working, and ministering as a Christian in one's home country. At times life goes smoothly, and at other times it does not:

> In the last six months on the mission field I have been slandered and sued by a mission employee. I have endured a strike by employees seeking higher wages. I have terminated a mission project sooner

than intended and laid off four faithful workers. I have suffered through government inspections and meetings. I have been awakened from sleep by a desperate plea to drive a woman to the hospital. I have been stranded in a broken down truck, and I have been separated from my family on numerous occasions.[9]

Although they focus on a common goal, teammates may not always agree on how to reach it. There may be personality differences to work through or differences in spiritual maturity. Sometimes team members come from different cultural backgrounds, making understanding and unity more challenging.

Despite the challenges of team dynamics, teams can also provide some of the missionary's most meaningful relationships. When Rose traveled to China because her daughter-in-law had given birth prematurely, she learned the comfort of good relationships with team members, not only for the missionary but also for POMs:

> Friend was too glib a word to apply to these people. They sacrificed, gave, journeyed, and helped despite their own lives, schedules, and needs. Sacrifice—that's the kind of love you find in a family.
>
> I returned home with a new common bond with our son and daughter-in-law: their friends became like family to me too. Now I'm genuinely thankful they care for and mean so much to each other. . . . I

haven't been replaced; I've been supported.

Good team members become the missionary's family on the field. "It's not uncommon for kids to refer to mission teammates as 'Aunt Jennifer' or 'Grandma Effie,' said Sue, a former missionary, "and it's a source of comfort and joy for missionary parents for their kids to have such surrogate relationships. It doesn't diminish or supplant blood relationships but rather expands the circle wider."

Moving between Two Cultures

Repeatedly moving between one's passport country and host country can be challenging. Missionaries frequently experience culture shock in reverse when returning to their home country on furlough or for a special occasion. "My worldview had been dramatically altered," wrote Nancy, a missionary. "I was no longer just an American, but I had also embraced some of the wonderful cultural aspects of the nation that had been my home for three years. My sense of humor had changed, my understanding of the importance of relationships had changed, and my idea of what was important in life and work had evolved."

Nancy related this experience of trying to buy cheese in the grocery store: "For the past three years overseas, buying cheese had not required a lot of thought. There was only one kind of cheese to buy in the store—block cheddar. . . . But now, to my amazement, I found myself standing in front of a whole wall of cheeses. I had to turn my head back and forth to see them all. . . . I was overwhelmed with the choices."[10]

Missionaries frequently find reentering their host country to be a challenge as well. A few days after my daughter returned to the field after the birth of her son, she included these words in a long note to friends: "I just started getting very sad. I'm wondering to myself, *Why am I doing this, again? Why am I here?* I know I'm still jet-lagging and stuff still isn't all put away and it's rainy and cloudy outside and my hormones aren't normal yet. . . . And that I need to give it some time."

Extended living outside of one's passport country changes people. When asked about changes in her life as a missionary, Stevanie wrote somewhat humorously, "Missionary life has made me far more humble than I used to be! I have fewer answers and more trust in the power of God than when we first went over. My parents probably think that is great!" Eileen said, "Being a missionary has made me think a lot more about heaven!" Jacque, another missionary, answered this way: "I'm a different person, completely. From my worldview all the way down to how I spend my days. My mother recognizes these changes—in fact, she has changed along with me. We discuss things of this matter often."

Other People's Expectations

The stereotypical missionary on furlough in dowdy, out-dated clothing and driving a rattletrap loaned car is no longer who most Christians expect to see when missionaries visit their church. Unfortunately, however, "a multitude of antiquated stereotypes and expectations linger, ready to nag the unsuspecting"

missionary, wrote B. Van Ochs (a pseudonym) in an article in
Evangelical Missions Quarterly.[11] Sadly, some missionaries still
receive the "gift" of used tea bags.

In his article, Van Ochs spotlights the unthinking expectations missionaries may encounter. Unsolicited advice is one. "For
whatever reason, people feel free to offer missionaries unsolicited
opinions in a way they wouldn't to their closest friends. Anything
is fair game—how to dress, how to educate children, how many
children to have, what to own, what type of medical care to
have, where to vacation, whether to marry, or about lifestyle
choices in general."

Another expectation Van Ochs identifies is that missionaries
should be grateful for anything they receive: "A friend on a missions committee related the story of a woman in the congregation
donating an old coat to the missions closet. Our friend asked the
woman if she would consider giving the coat to her daughter,
and she answered, 'No, it's out of style.' So Bennie asked, 'Well,
why would you give it to a missionary?' The unspoken answer
was 'Because they should be grateful to have it.' Bennie told her
to go buy a new coat and donate it, which she did."

Other expectations missionaries encounter, according
to Van Ochs, include the expectations that they will always
"rough it," that ministry is conducted in specific ways, and that
success is always measured in terms of conversions to Christ.
"The point is that it is difficult to quantify ministry," he wrote.
"Especially when the traditional yardstick question for mea-
suring 'success' is 'How many people have you led to Christ?'
Well, personally, none, but I've helped others do it. Does that

count?"

At the opposite end of the expectations yardstick are Christians in the passport country who put missionaries on a pedestal, Van Ochs says. "While some feel free to criticize missionaries, others elevate them to a special status. The inherent danger of the superspiritual classification is that it perpetuates the stereotypical inability of missionaries to be real people."

Being placed on a spiritual pedestal, unable to be real, creates problems for missionaries. "You know you aren't up there," said Daniela. "If you're struggling spiritually, are you a failure?" Belinda added, "On the other hand, you might be having a great time, having fun being here, even if it's hard, but you wonder if people will stop praying if you tell them that." Doug agrees: "Most missionaries end up viewing [their work] as not all outcomes-geared . . . but there's an ambiguity and intangibleness to deal with. There's a pressure in our newsletters to 'sell it.'"

Even POMs can hold their own set of expectations. Doug said: "One thing my mom worried about early on was how we would parent and what risks we would be willing to take with the kids. What brought me to missions was a kind of radicalness, exposure to radical people, risk takers. I feel less radical now. I'm a parent and concerned about my kids. The first year, I prayed that we would stay healthy so God could prove to my mom that He would take care of us and take care of the kids. There was a tension of having to prove this, in a way."

MK and TCK Realities

We've already noted the stresses of moving back and forth between two cultures. Children who are raised on the mission field (missionary kids, or MKs) experience that stress somewhat differently than their parents. They experience life as Third Culture Kids (TCKs)—able to relate to both their parents' culture and their host culture but not fully identifying with either one. (In 1999, the groundbreaking book *Third Culture Kids: The Experience of Growing Up Among Worlds,* by David C. Pollock and Ruth E. Van Reken, greatly expanded our understanding of the term *Third Culture Kid,* first used by researcher Dr. Ruth Hill Useem in the 1960s.)

A Question of Identity

"Our culture shapes who we are and how we understand, interpret, and relate to our environment," wrote John Larsen, a Christian counselor (and an MK himself). But TCKs do not have a simple answer to the question "Where are you from?" Larsen says:

> Being asked "Where are you from?" can sometimes be distressing to MKs. A response requires telling one's story, not just naming a place. MKs may not be comfortable sharing their story with the person inquiring. The question also evokes a bit of pain involving confusion about belonging. . . . MKs are not able to meet the psychological need to be rooted in a community of persons similar to

themselves. The longing to belong and a painful sense of not belonging are ever present.[12]

In general, TCKs are most comfortable with other TCKs, and they experience the most distress and difficulty adjusting when they enter or reenter the home culture of their parents. Kim Holland, an MK who is now a psychiatric nurse practitioner, described some of the difficulties like this:

MKs feel comfortable being different in a foreign country. They are supposed to be different. They may be the only blonde among their black-haired classmates or the tallest student in their class, but feeling lost in the place they thought was home [their parent's culture] is very unsettling. . . . MKs can be afraid of losing their identity in their home culture. They may refuse to learn the new ways or adjust to changes. All of these conflicts may be acted out as anger, rebellion, or isolation from peers.[13]

TCKs and MKs may also be affected by spending substantial time away from their parents at boarding schools at a young age, especially if they are not given adequate support in processing the pain and distress of the separation.

TCKs do have many strengths, of course, that develop through their cross-cultural experiences. Larsen notes that they can be resourceful, adaptable people with an adventurous spirit and a great sense of humor. In addition, he says, "Multilingual fluency, a high degree of global-mindedness, and broad perspectives seen in most TCKs equip them for careers in the growing global economy." But he notes that many TCKs do not value these traits.

What POMs Can Do for TCKs

Missionary parents can help their children learn the art of making new friends, encourage their children to learn about their home culture just as they would a foreign culture, and they can talk to their children openly about the issues they encounter.[14] POMs have a role to play too. If we maintain a close relationship with our grandchildren while they are on the field, we can be a mentor for them whenever they reenter their home culture, as the following quote from a missionary poignantly makes clear. The following principles apply to grandfathers and grandsons, to grandmothers and granddaughters, and to grandparents from any culture, although the writer is American:

> I appreciate my mother and mother-in-law more each time we are back in the U.S. They are more important in the lives of my daughters than they would be if we lived a "normal" American life, and I think we all realize that. Because we live our lives in a cross-cultural setting, they make a big contribution by giving our children a kind of foundation in American culture, in a loving, wholesome way. Our lives are characterized by a high level of mobility, and yet Grandma's house, Grandma's hugs, Grandma's cooking are a constant in our daughters' memories.

When the time comes for each girl to "move" back to the U.S. for college and career, that place of stability will still be there, Lord willing. And one of the biggest challenges for Third Culture Kids is that elusive sense of identity, of being able to construct an answer to the question "Who are you and where are you from?" Their grandmas are one of the most significant resources for them in the search for identity. The last time we were in the U.S., my mom spent many hours teaching our daughters sewing skills, and they worked on special projects together. This is a part of her heritage that she is passing on to them. My mom-in-law sat paging through old photo albums with them, telling family stories and highlighting the particular characteristics of relatives that carry on through the generations. The grandmas are the storehouses of the family memories that can be so important to our TCKs as they try to find their own identities.[15]

Churches can also play a role in addressing TCK issues. Connie noted proudly that her grandchildren, Brady and Amber, who went to the field as preteens, were able to travel home to Pennsylvania each summer during high school to visit friends, thanks to the generosity of their sending church.

Worth It All

Despite the challenges of their lives, missionaries press on.

They find satisfaction in doing what God has asked, in seeing growth in themselves and others, and in helping others find Christ.

Personal Growth

Many missionaries discover that God is working in them as much as in the people to whom they minister. "God allows things to come up, in you or from the past, to let you deal with them, to grow and be healed," Cindi explained. "Your usual defenses don't work here anymore—you don't have the same escapes. Things are more stripped down." Cindi's husband, Mark, agrees. "God is the one working and I just join in. God is doing a work in me, and others I am in contact with are affected."

In an article for the online magazine *Women of the Harvest*, Joy wrote: "As I look back over these past two years, I understand now that God sent me overseas to begin healing me emotionally. It has been a hard process for me, my husband, and my children, and I am saddened at the pain they went through on my account. Yet at the same time I am very thankful for the transforming work of the Holy Spirit in my life and the freedom I now have in Christ."[16]

Missionaries deepen their dependence and reliance on God. Ask them to tell you about the times God intervened dramatically on their behalf—they won't lack stories to tell. Ask how their dependence on God has changed how they view themselves. "I've changed in my view of my own necessity," said Doug. "Missionaries go to the field to change the world. . . . You find out that . . . there is little you can do, and that really God is doing it. I'm just to be obedient; the results aren't up to me."

One Thing That Matters

Despite the ambiguities, uncertainties, and challenges, missionaries affirm again and again that what they do is worth it—worth the sacrifices, the hardships, and the separations from friends and family. "In the back of all our minds, ours and our families," said Doug, "is the question 'Is it worth being here?' I've decided that it can be just one thing that matters. We have a neighbor who didn't know God, and now he does. If I can help him grow solid, that matters."

A veteran missionary wrote:

> Many challenges are involved in missionary life, but many joys also come along the way. One of the great joys is that the consciousness of God's faithfulness in all situations becomes ever more precious. The sense of God's presence and grace becomes ever more acute. A second joy is getting to know some wonderful persons who radiate a commitment to their Lord, an experience which crosses racial and cultural lines. Thirdly, the missionary comes to know in a unique way the meaning of the holy, catholic [worldwide, universal] church. And, to mention just one more joy, this missionary activity gives the missionary a deep personal satisfaction. To God be the praise![17]

Parents as Partners

In chapter 6 we discussed the value of learning as much as possible during prefield preparation about your missionary's host country and work. Such learning is even more important now, and it's never too late to begin.

Also learn about specific individuals your missionary has contact with. Ask questions. Paula said, "So few of our children's supporters and friends will really listen to them and their stories. I find it is of greatest support that I know the names of the people they are talking about on the field and interact with them as they tell their stories. Pay close attention to what they are saying and ask lots of questions."[18]

Parents can also learn about missionary life and work through books, movies, newsletters, and websites (see the list of suggested resources at the back of this book); by attending mission conferences and conventions; by participating in sending-agency events; and by visiting the field (see chapter 13). The Perspectives course, offered by the U.S. Center for World Mission at various locations in the United States and around the world, is also an excellent way to gain a deeper understanding of God's ultimate purpose in the world.

The more we learn, the more we are willing to understand, empathize, listen, and pray, the more we support our missionary and add action to our parental blessing. In turn, we are also blessed.

TOGETHER AGAIN

Satisfying Furloughs

Parents can help their children by letting them do what they must do, and making the time that they are able to spend together a true celebration of love and family.

—a missionary

"There they are!" You spot your missionary in the throng of people walking into the toward baggage claim from the arrival gates. What relief and gratitude! How wonderful it is to welcome missionaries home, to see them again, to spend time face-to-face instead of on Skype! I (Diane) experienced the joy of furlough several times during the years I was a POM.

Also called home service or home assignment, furlough is time for missionaries to recuperate from the stresses of cross-cultural living and service. It's also time for them to do missions motivation and mobilization (sometimes called deputation) as well as to debrief and strategize with their sending agency or church. It's often time to visit supporting churches and to search for additional financial support.

The timing and length of a furlough vary according to the field of service and the policies of the sending organization. Traditionally, missionaries came home for a year at a time after several years on the field. Today some missionaries enjoy shorter furloughs on a more frequent basis. "Eras have changed," said Heidi, a missionary who also grew up on the field. "Missionaries used to leave and seldom return. In my own family we were gone three years and home for one. Now it's pretty much up to us."

It's tempting to view furlough strictly as a returning, but Alice, a POM, has a different view: "All could define furlough as an uprooting, which may or may not include work, further education, workshops, retreats and conferences, travel, family time, grandparent time, sibling and cousin time, weddings, funerals, and vacation." Not only are the missionaries uprooted from what is now their home as they return to their passport country, but parents and extended family also can experience an uprooting of sorts as normal routines and living experiences give way to maximize time with the missionary and grandchildren. Clearly, knowing what to expect and making plans wisely is a good path to follow.

Plan Ahead

"Before your missionaries arrive home," said Alice, "pray and communicate as much as possible to help their time at home be profitable for God's kingdom and your precious children." Try to anticipate your missionary's furlough responsibilities.

"Parents need to understand that though it is a time of rest, it also comes with a lot of responsibility," said Karen, a missionary. "I think my mother has a pretty good handle on what furlough is about." Stevanie, also a missionary, said, "If their children need to raise their own support and maintain that support base, parents need to understand that process and have an idea of what it will look like for their children to do that while they are back home."

As furlough begins, missionaries need respite—time to regroup after packing and traveling through multiple time zones. Dr. Ronald L. Koteskey, member-care consultant for New Hope International Ministries, wrote about reentry, the process of returning to one's passport country: "In one sense many people are still transitioning for several days or weeks after they arrive home. They unpack their suitcases long before they unpack their minds."[1]

Whatever can be done before arriving to settle housing, transportation, finances, and children's schooling eases the reentry process for our missionaries. Allan, a POM, observed, "Coming home presents significant challenges, and calls for creative travel and living arrangements."

Housing

Depending on the length of the furlough and the policies of the sending organization, missionaries may rent a house or apartment or campus housing, or they may live with or near their parents. Some organizations require missionaries on furlough to live in a specific location.

Sending churches may take responsibility for arranging housing. Or if the missionary will locate near parents, they may provide housing in various ways for all or part of the furlough. One family parked a large motor home on their property for their missionary and family to live in, enjoying the benefits of living close, yet with private space for all. Another family purchased a condo near their home that they keep available for their missionary during furloughs. Still other parents share their home with their missionary. When we moved several years ago, we kept furlough in mind as we searched for a house with a finished lower level where our daughter and son-in-law could live during furlough, providing plenty of space for all of us and privacy for everyone too.

Transportation

Someone in your congregation may be willing to loan a vehicle for your missionary to use during furlough, or POMs can sometimes help with this need. "I have a full-sized conversion van that I hardly need anymore," said Ken, "but it stays in the garage most of the time for two years, waiting for my daughter and her family to come home for the summer. They have five children, so the van does wonderfully well for a family of seven. When they arrived this year, I was able to be there with the van, not only greeting them but propelling them along for a successful summer on home leave."

For shorter furloughs, Allan had a different suggestion: "We have purchased a car prior to the family coming that is safe and reliable but also has good potential for resale. After they return to their mission assignment, we sell the car, usually for the same price we bought it two months earlier. Reliable transportation was available at no cost other than the gas for miles traveled."

Finances

Missionaries can be financially stretched while on furlough, especially if they don't anticipate and plan for higher living costs. "The cost of living [on furlough] may be more or less than in the host country," explained Sue, a former missionary. "Urban Mexico City prices are vastly different than rural African prices for housing and food, for example. So that will determine how much money is needed for furlough expenses. Some agencies give a furlough adjustment based on an index that is used globally for determining costs of living."

Sometimes "work funds" (as opposed to personal salary funds) can be applied to furlough expenses, Sue said, and sometimes newly committed support, raised on furlough, can also be applied to those expenses. Usually a portion of work funds and personal salary, however, must continue to be applied in the host country while the missionary is away. Missionaries may need to leave money behind to pay substitute English teachers, for example, or to pay rent on their apartment or home.

Occasionally a church or an individual drops financial support during a furlough, thinking the money isn't needed while the missionary is at home. "Actually, we needed more money, not less," said Lynn, a POM and former missionary.

Furlough can be more expensive than regular day-to-day living for POMs as well. If the missionary's family lives with parents, costs for groceries, gasoline, and utilities increase. Missionaries are likely to contribute to these costs but may be limited in what they can pay. If POMs travel to where the missionary is living during furlough, there may be the cost of airfare, a rental car, accommodations, and food. In either case POMs are likely to want to "go and do" more than usual, especially if there are grandchildren. Starting to save now for the next furlough can help relieve some of the financial stress.

Children's Schooling

How missionaries handle their children's schooling while on furlough can vary. Sue, also quoted above, explained a number of the options missionaries have:

> Most missionaries tend to stick with whatever they do on the field. If homeschooling, there's lots of freedom for kids to stay with parents as they travel, but it's sometimes hard to keep up with the curriculum because of the travel. Its harder, but doable, to *start* homeschooling on furlough, or homeschool *only* on furloughs, and some do so in order to have the flexibility. Others feel their kids may need or enjoy the higher degree of social interaction in a classroom setting, along with the

break it provides for the homeschooling parent. However, this has its own set of issues when the children aren't used to the [school] system. . . . Some countries start their school year in January, or the spring, so the two worlds don't mesh well when going back and forth!

MKs attending school in their passport country may face issues relating to being Third Culture Kids, as we've noted earlier. "Each kind of schooling has its own set of challenges, but none is insurmountable," said Sue. "It's important [for missionaries] to keep talking to their kids (or for POMs to talk to grandkids) and let them express both the good and bad parts of their school adjustment. They can love and hate it at the same time—as with other parts of the furlough experience."

Time Together

Whether your missionary lives with you, nearby, or a distance away during furlough, there are ways to ensure that the time you have together is a fruitful, satisfying time.

Longer furloughs may make this easier to accomplish, of course. "We had plenty of time with family," wrote Sherry, "a whole year in the States, so we didn't feel rushed. We got together with our parents several times, since we weren't living in the same town or state."

Alice expressed the need to take a flexible, positive, creative attitude toward furlough. "Before anything is planned or put on the calendar," she said, "always check with the missionaries for their approval, consideration, and convenience." Another POM had this advice: "Don't think about them going back. Just enjoy every moment that you have with them. It is a very special time, and one you will not forget."

Travel

Parents who are able and willing to travel to their missionary's home on furlough can be a blessing for everyone. As one missionary shared, "We have one set of parents (they are semiretired) who try very hard to rearrange their lives while we are home on furlough to maximize our time together. That's really wonderful."

"Having our parents come for significant events in our kids' lives has meant a lot to us," said Tina. "It's huge. While we are home, they have come—traveling seven hours—for the girls' birthday parties and school concerts. They have kept our daughters some too and sent us on dates."

"I think we maximize, or maybe the word is optimize, the face-to-face time when they are home," wrote Ken. "Usually my daughter and her family spend a week with me in Missouri. Their epicenter of supporting churches is in Iowa, and they have good friends who let them live in their home in Iowa Falls. I know their church visitation schedule, and I usually manage to catch up with them at a couple of those. Other times I just go and spend some more time with them at their summer home in Iowa Falls."

If your missionary and grandchildren will be traveling to visit supporting churches on weekends, maximize your time together by doing what Jim and Rita did—they went too! Other families enjoy vacationing together during furlough. A relaxed environment and plenty of unscheduled time away from phones and e-mails can contribute to wonderful times and talks together. This family time can mean as much to missionaries as to POMs. "We like to plan some kind of special event," said Stevanie, a missionary on furlough. "This year it is Christmas, family-reunion style. All my siblings, their kids, cousins and their kids, aunts and uncles—we are coming in from all over the country."

Everyday Life

Not all furlough time can be filled with major events. While we did plan special family events during furlough, we also greatly enjoyed doing everyday things together. Some of my favorite memories with my daughter are organizing kitchen cupboards, planning a party menu, going out to lunch, and shopping. My husband and my son-in-law were sure to take in an action-packed movie at least once every visit.

Missionaries also appreciate getting to just "do life" together with you. Heidi, from a missionary family spread out over the globe, said, "With my family we tend to all gather for a few days. It is great, but I sometimes wish I could spend more time with my sister especially. She has children too, and we could do things together." My son-in-law observed, "Sometimes it's nice to have more intentional times together—acting like 'You're back!'—and sometimes it's nice just to allow the natural ebb and flow of life together."

It's healthy to allow space in your time together. Everyone needs a break sometimes, parents as well as missionaries. "Our time with family tends to be so concentrated," said Doug, "but my parents can't spend all their time with the kids or they wear out. There's also a tension because you can only talk deep for so long. At some point you've got to just live, and do chores."

Intentionality

In chapter 7 we mentioned that sometimes POMs must ask for the time they'd like to spend with their missionaries in the days or weeks before departure. That's true about furlough too.

Although flexibility and acceptance are keys to a successful furlough, there are times when intentionally asking for what you'd like is also important. For example, POMs can encourage the missionary's extended family members, such as grandparents, siblings, and cousins, to save vacation days at work to use during furlough for special times and events. A little forethought and speaking up can prevent a lot of disappointment for many.

Also, encourage your spouse to plan how he or she would like to spend time with the missionary. In many families, one parent is closer to the missionary than the other. Fathers, for example, tend to let their wives be more involved with their daughters. During furlough visits, however, these fathers may feel left out as their wives and daughters happily make plans and spend time together.

I always encouraged my husband to be intentional with his time when our daughter was on furlough, whether simply "hanging out" more when she was around (proximity provides more opportunities for interaction) or making specific plans with Sheila to spend time together. My husband can attest that both of these tactics worked well.

Sharing a Home Together

Not all POMs want to or are able to live under one roof with their children during furlough. But many do, and missionaries may welcome this opportunity. "When we first toyed with the idea of living in my parents' basement apartment while back on furlough," said Stevanie, "my mother was really nervous about the idea, not wanting to interfere with our family, not wanting to put out so much effort for us that she became resentful. We talked it through and tried it. We both loved it and have done it this way ever since."

Another missionary offered her thoughts on multigenerational living: "We lived with my mom this year," wrote Karen, "and I am seeing more and more the value of missionary children living with their parents rather than taking the expense of setting up two homes, one overseas and one here, if the parents and children can get along. My husband and I know other missionaries who have done this successfully, and we are beginning to explore the idea of the multigenerational family for the future when we return to the U.S."

More people in the house mean more noise and more clutter, especially if you have grandchildren. It's best to talk about dividing household responsibilities right at the beginning. Lynn, a former missionary and now a POM, suggested designating one or two rooms as "kid free" rooms—off-limits to grandchildren.

Then POMs have space of their own that stays neat to use as a retreat when needed. And many POMs say they need a balance between time spent with the missionary and grandchildren and time for their own routines, friends, and spouse.

Living together increases the possibilities of doing normal things together. Stevanie, who lives each furlough with her family in her parents' basement apartment, said, "We have our own space, but we are there for all the spontaneous, wonderful things that happen. We talk whenever we want, and have many more chances to do it. We are able to do some work around their place, which makes me feel very good. I understand that this would not work for everyone; I am so glad that it has worked for us."

Furlough Challenges

Parents sometimes think that when their missionary is on furlough everything will be normal again. But what once was normal may not be any longer. Be aware of the challenges furlough presents so you can successfully navigate the sometimes choppy waters.

Dealing with Changes

Life as a missionary changes people. I could see this during my daughter Sheila's first furlough. She and I agreed I would buy her running shoes for her birthday, but Sheila, who had always loved to shop, was not looking forward to going to the mall. Hmm.

So we planned a quick-in, quick-out shopping trip. We looked at running shoes in three stores, and then Sheila tried on a few pairs in the third store, where we made our purchase. She needed to find one or two other things before going back to the field, so we hit one clothing store on our way out of the mall. Then Sheila said, "Okay, Mom, that's it. Let's go home." She had grown accustomed to the smaller shops and simpler product selection in her host country. The abundance where she had grown up now felt overwhelming and to a degree wasteful and ostentatious.

In *Peter's Wife,* an e-newsletter for missionary women, Debbie wrote that her first furloughs back to the United States were hard: "Everyone seemed so spoiled, wasteful, ethnocentric, inward-focused, superficial—you get the idea! I really struggled with a bad attitude and was very critical of my fellow American Christians and their lifestyles."[2]

Missions mobilizer Neal Pirolo wrote in his book *Serving as Senders* that missionaries reentering their home culture face stresses in eight areas.[3] Most of the stresses he lists are apt to affect missionaries on furlough too. Missionaries may be stunned by the wealth, consumer mindset, busyness, and casual attitude toward missions of people at home. "My perspective on the world, my worldview, has changed, and my kids have also been impacted," said Mark, a missionary. "What do we really need to live? Was how we lived before what we *needed* or something else?"

Many missionaries feel that home is now located in their host country. They may at times have difficulty expressing themselves in their native language because they have begun to think in their new, acquired tongue. Politically, they may view the world with new eyes. "I identify here now," said one missionary on the field, "not necessarily with what our home country's policies are toward our host country. I see the impact of those policies."

As a result of these stresses, missionaries may feel alienated at home and begin to express condemning attitudes toward their home government, home church, and maybe even their parents. And they may not be aware this is happening, said Lynn, based on her experience as a missionary. "Sometimes it's a shock to be 'at home' but not feel at home," she explained.

Faced with these kinds of reactions in our returning missionary children, we may be tempted to be defensive. But the best response is calm acceptance and a humble willingness to try to understand. That also draws us closer to our missionaries, rather than holding us apart.

Relationships with Siblings

As we stated in the introduction, we've purposely limited the scope of this book to parents of missionaries, but we realize that siblings and extended family members of missionaries also grieve and must find ways to adjust and thrive. One aspect of furlough that can be challenging for POMs, however, involves siblings and their interactions with the missionary.

When siblings are close and enjoy each other's company, our parent hearts feel joy and contentment. Other times, sibling interactions can bring pain. One POM mother shared these words from her journal, written during the first two months of a yearlong furlough: "There seems to be no wiggle room here. Expectations are not met. There has been an unexpected change in opinions or philosophy. The sibling of childhood has become 'someone else.' Whatever the case, the relationship is deemed close to dead and buried. . . . I see the pain. I *feel* the pain. I see what appears to be an unfortunate lack of interest on the part of the stay-at-home sibling, but as a mother I understand that it's actually insecurity at work."

At times like these, I found it helpful to remind myself of my love for each of my children and to look for opportunities to speak the truth to each one in love, as Ephesians 4:15 commands.

Unmet Ideals

Flexibility and grace are two attributes to apply liberally to all aspects of furlough. Despite your best planning, things will not always go as you hope. One POM found that although the first furlough went well, the second did not. "Our good intentions and months of careful planning have mostly backfired," she wrote in her journal. "Who meets them at the airport? How long do they stay with which family as they become reacquainted? How do we have 'quality time' (I've come to hate that phrase!)? Which scenario—A, B, or C—would work the best for everyone? Months and months of praying and planning have needed tweaking."

On my daughter and son-in-law's first furlough, near the end of a wonderful family vacation with us, my son-in-law received a call from his mother—his younger brother had died suddenly and tragically. The remaining few weeks of furlough were devoted to my son-in-law's family, and rightly so, but this wasn't the way I had planned for furlough to end. God's grace gave me the ability to flex and accept others' needs as far above my own. When Sheila and Scoggins arrived back in Cincinnati a few days before their departure, we were able to squeeze in a celebration of her birthday and mine.

At times like these, POMs must rely on God to show us how to respond! Prayer, journaling, physical exercise, and honest discussion with close friends are some of the best activities to help us cope.

Giving the Gift of Encouragement

What missionaries say they need on furlough from their parents (and from extended family members) more than anything else is encouragement. And there are so many ways POMs can give their missionaries the gift of encouragement during this time.

Ask Questions and Listen to the Answers

Former missionaries Edward and Linda Speyers wrote in a guide to caring for missionaries, "Be aware that missionaries may feel 'out of it' when they return to their home culture after a long absence. Friendliness and a listening ear go a long way in alleviating reverse culture shock."[4] Another missionary, Sherry, advised, "The biggest thing parents can do is to listen to their children talk about their experiences overseas, to ask questions, and to look at their pictures. Sometimes families show the least interest of anyone, and that is really discouraging."

Give Your Missionary Time to Adjust

Many missionaries vouch for the importance of reserving the first few days or weeks of furlough for getting over jet lag and easing back into their passport country. And, although asking questions and listening to your missionary's stories are important, some missionaries don't want to talk right away. They've gone through a long process of disengagement from the field to make this trip home; now they want to be present where they are and reengage in their home country.

Help Arrange a Gathering

A drop-in style gathering of friends can be a great encouragement to your missionary and is something parents can help arrange. One missionary wrote: "This takes care of many visits and meals that they just don't have time to see to. . . . Another great thing is to arrange a get-together of their Bible college or seminary friends. (I enjoyed this the most of all things on our first furlough.)"[5] POMs have also arranged girlfriend lunches and reunions with cousins for their missionaries. Trying to see many small groups and individual supporters can be physically, mentally, and emotionally draining. If your church is involved in sending your missionary, one big reception, cookout, or dinner at the church allows your missionary to give an update and receive prayer, and POMs can take a role in planning an event of this kind too.

Learn about Your Missionary's Host Country

This can help you be an encouragement during furlough and when the missionary is on the field. "Study the country in which your children live and watch for articles and shows about it," said Susan, a POM. "It will help you understand what your kids are living through, as well as show them that you have an interest in where they live."

Be Careful How You Talk about the Future

Parents' words have an impact, missionaries advise, either positive or negative. "It is very discouraging to have parents and relatives beg you to stay in the States," said Sherry. "'There are needs here, too, you know' type of comments are frustrating and annoying." My son-in-law offered this perspective:

> A lot of people and some family have asked, "When have you guys thought about coming back?" and questions like that. Those kinds of questions are really hard, because we really felt that it wasn't our decision in the first place to go over. We really felt it was God saying "Go over." So I'd like to talk about what God is doing. Questions like "Has He shared with you that this is going to end soon?"—I appreciate that kind of question. It takes me out of it. Otherwise it's like I have chosen to live far, far away. And that's not the case at all.

Think from Your Missionary's Point of View

Extending yourself by learning to think from your missionary's point of view encourages him or her. This doesn't mean that all your routines must change or that you must assume all caretaking and household responsibilities if you are living together. But don't insist on everything being done your way. For example, Tina shared that missionaries and grandchildren may not want to travel even short distances when they visit POMs:

> "Can I take you somewhere?" may not be the best suggestion. In our situation, our girls especially prefer to just be left at home in their comfort zone rather than traveling again. To help this, parents can come to the missionary and do things close to their home for a few hours, if possible. This same concept may apply to going out to eat, when the kids have to be on their best behavior. Better for grandparents to get carryout and have a picnic with a blanket on the living room floor, from my kids' perspective.

Connect with Your Grandchildren

Deepening your relationship with your grandchildren by spending time with them is one of the most practical helps you can give your missionary—and it's one of the best gifts you can give yourself. Spending time together is much more important than giving elaborate gifts, and it leaves good memories. Tina, quoted above, also shared that her children "had a blast blowing

bubbles with their grandpa and walking his dog. They appreciated having Grandma read to them and cuddle on the sofa." If
you are able, offer to keep your grandchildren for a week each
furlough so that they really get to know you, and you them.
"Our parents telling our kids stories from our own childhoods
and their own childhoods has helped to give our kids a sense of
rootedness," said Tina.

If your grandchildren have been raised from birth on the
field, you might be surprised by some of their behaviors. Paula
wrote:

> We worked among a tribal people whose church
> services tended to be long but informal events
> where people came and went, where services were
> in various homes, where moms would feed their
> children a bowl of cereal while the service was going
> on, and where the children were allowed to roam
> around. Your grandkids may not be used to sitting
> still in a church service for an hour and may not
> understand a lot of what is happening at church.
> Put yourself in their shoes. How do you think you
> might behave if you were raised in the jungles of
> Brazil and knew little else![6]

As a loving grandparent, you naturally want to spend time
with your grandchildren, but don't underestimate the value and
benefit to your grandchildren of having a relationship with you.
Take time to understand the Third Culture Kid phenomenon
that impacts children who grow up on the mission field and

how to be a stability point in your grandchildren's lives (see chapter 8). Also be sure to read chapter 10 on grandparenting long-distance.

Make the Missionary's Marriage Relationship a Priority

If your missionary has a spouse and children, "another thing parents can do is offer to babysit the grandkids so the missionary couple can have some time to go out alone," said Sherry. "This can help the couple as well as cement the relationship between the grandparents and grandchildren." Alice agreed: "Respite for the married couple is an added blessing of furlough. Send the couple off for a weekend. Many missionaries do not have pastors and need this time to renew and regroup. A session with a counselor or a marriage enrichment weekend is appreciated too."

Be Teachable and Prayerful

Reflecting on the experience of sending his daughter to the mission field shortly after college, one father wrote, "I have discovered that some of our best work as parents has been accomplished with our two adult children. We all discovered together the secret to knowing God's will; it's knowing God intimately."[7] POMs have tremendous opportunities to learn and grow and thereby to be an example to their children. Proverbs 17:6 says, "Parents are the pride of their children" (NIV), and I want my daughters to be proud of me!

Humility and a desire to learn and grow are parental assets that encourage our missionaries. Wrote one POM whose missionary family was living with her while on furlough, "I have been convicted of many of my selfish, sinful attitudes as well as things I had been doing that upset my daughter. We had some pretty honest talks." Another POM who was experiencing conflict with her family on furlough wrote, "I am praying to be a learner during this time. Back to the Lord's classroom yet again."

Saying Good-Bye Again

The time comes when furlough is winding down and the date for returning to the field is set. After a successful furlough with plenty of wonderful family time, preparing for another departure may seem a daunting task. "Hello, good-bye. Hello, good-bye. Sometimes I think that describes my life," said Carole shortly after her son and his family returned to the field after a furlough. Over the years, although we become more experienced at saying good-bye, most POMs find it is never an easy thing to face.

Missionaries experience this emotional seesaw too. "Going back to the field is never easy and never simple; it's complicated and full of different emotions," my son-in-law said. Another missionary shared, "I begin to count my blessings, to cement in my memory the good things that have happened on furlough. I admit to having to bolster my courage before returning to face stressful living conditions. I get tired and stressed trying to take care of all the last-minute details."

A group gathering to allow the missionaries to say good-bye to many people at one time may be helpful at the end of a furlough. My daughter and son-in-law hosted about two dozen friends and supporters in our home one evening shortly before their last furlough ended. After dessert and time to talk, they gave everyone printouts with photos of all the friends and co-workers they would see on their return. They talked about their work and their desire to connect people in their passport country with the work they were doing and the individuals they were serving. The group joined together in prayer for all of these concerns.

This special evening was also a baby dedication. Our first grandchild was born on this furlough. Now just seven weeks old, he would be traveling to the field with his mom and dad. Both of them spoke about their concerns and desires for their son, and then everyone gathered around the family, laid hands on them, and prayed. One of their friends prayed for us as POMs and for other family members remaining behind. It was a very personal, very special occasion.

That evening's events represent for me so many aspects of a satisfying furlough, which is complex and requires hard work on everyone's part. As POMs we support and participate and are blessed, and our children don't overlook our efforts. One missionary summed up the gratitude she and her husband experience this way: "We get some sort of blessing before each return, knowing that our families are behind us. Yes, we know they sacrifice to send us and their grandchildren off again, but to know that this is something they do willingly makes all the difference in the world to us."

STAYING CONNECTED

Practical, inspirational insights for creating and keeping strong family bonds across the miles.

A PIECE OF MYSELF

10

Building Bridges to Grandchildren Far Away

There could be no greater grandparents than my folks. The hard work invested has resulted in great love between them and their distant grandkids. I am sure they would say that the effort was worth it.

—a missionary

With their free-flowing love, playful spirits, beauty, honesty, and innocence, grandchildren possess an amazing capacity to enchant and hook the hearts of their grandparents.

Grandchildren often transform previously dignified and serious-minded adults into rather amusing personalities who scout for any opportunity to show pictures and tell tales about their little darlings. Some of the tales are even entertaining, like Grandma Evelyn's story about two-year-old Robert's strategic lunchtime prayer: "Dear God, please help Mommy stop telling me what to do!"

Grandkids get grandparents to spend inordinate amounts of money and go to great lengths to delight them. Grandparents say things like, "If I'd known grandchildren were this much fun, I'd have had them first!" and, "My grandkids are my reward for not killing my kids." Grandkids help grandparents feel connected to the future, and they even go home when grandparents grow tired! Clearly, being with grandkids brings great joy to grandparents.

Conversely, separation from grandchildren usually brings great pain, especially when grandchildren live on a distant mission field. My (Cheryl's) research suggests POMs feel more negative about separation from grandkids than separation from their missionary. One nationally known church leader, grandpa, and adamant missions supporter told us through tears, "I'm afraid I won't know my grandchildren and they won't know me." A grandma said, "Most of the time, when I tell someone my family has just left for the mission field, their response is 'How wonderful!'—except for the grandmas. . . . They identify with the enormous feeling of loss."

As a POM, you may experience uncertainty about how growing up on a mission field will affect your impressionable grandchildren. One POM grandma was relieved when she got to know a well-adjusted young adult who had grown up on the mission field. "I met a delightful MK who works with an agency here in the U.S.," she said. "What an encouragement to toss the anxiety and know our grandchildren can grow up emotionally healthy and connected to our family and culture, even if they do only visit every four years."

Most grandparents regard separation from grandkids as the

hardest part of the POM experience. Janice told us the pain does not ease over time, and Dawn noted that a POM's grief over separation does not reflect a lack of support for missions: "My folks were mission minded and my in-laws were missionaries themselves. I say all that to say this—it doesn't make it any easier to be away from your grandchildren just because you believe in missions and are even happy that they are on the mission field."

Though we consistently encounter POMs who agonize over separation from grandchildren, we also hear a great deal about the close, fun relationships some POMs manage to build with their grandchildren far away. Their success stories prove that family members don't have to live close to enjoy emotional close-ness. One dad reported feeling closer to his grandchildren living on a mission field thousands of miles away than those living a distance of only a few hundred miles.

Still, geographical distance can threaten emotional ties. In order to prevent emotional distance from developing, POMs must become proactive and work to build connections across the miles. Lori, a missionary, wrote, "My parents really work diligently to maintain closeness to their grandchildren halfway around the world. . . . They've done an incredible job! . . . The hard work invested has resulted in great love between them and their distant grandkids."

If you want to connect with grandkids living on the mission field, we encourage you to believe in your ability to grow close relationships despite the distance and decide to do so. Negative beliefs like "They're too far away" and "I don't count" will make you passive and cause you to miss out on what could be great relationships. Then, learn how to grandparent in healthy ways and develop some creative methods for staying in touch with your grandchildren on the mission field.

A Healthy Grandparent Model

Some grandparents cause problems for the entire family by distorting the appropriate grandparent role. Since many of us grew up in families that failed to provide a healthy model for grandparents, we will take time here to describe the nature of healthy grandparenting.

Grandparents as Nonparents

Dr. Vietta Keith Richardson, a clinical psychologist, encourages grandparents to stay out of the parenting business.[1] "You don't need to play the heavy in your grandchild's life," she says. "Let parents worry about stuff like holding kids accountable and applying discipline." She urges grandparents to respect the parents' prerogative to set rules, talk to teachers, intervene in sibling disputes, and decide what children can and can't have. She adds, "Staying out of the parent role gives you freedom to be the 'icing' on your grandchild's cake. Rather than worrying and taking on responsibility that belongs to the parents, you can simply concentrate on loving and nurturing your grandkids."

As a grandparent, you may struggle to avoid the parent role, Dr. Richardson acknowledges. It takes self-control to sit quietly while your son or daughter fights needlessly with a grandchild over something inconsequential, like eating *all* his vegetables.

You may catch yourself rolling your eyes in the face of parental rules that seem pointless and annoying. But Dr. Richardson cautions, "The old joke about grandparents and grandkids sharing a common enemy, the parents, should be held lightly." She condones slipping a grandchild a piece of candy on occasion for fun (if you have a positive relationship with the parents) but warns against ever going around the parents in any way that seriously undermines their authority. "Grandma and Grandpa should not say yes after the parents have said no."

When intervention seems called for, Dr. Richardson suggests thinking twice before addressing parents. If you decide to proceed, she recommends approaching parents with respect by acknowledging their authority and their freedom not to follow your advice.

POMs need not feel inconsequential in the lives of their grandchildren just because they choose to heed Dr. Richardson's advice and stay out of the parenting role. With a vision for grandparenting well, you can make a positive, life-changing difference in your grandchild's life!

Grandparents as Cherishers

As a grandparent, you can minister to the tender and malleable hearts of your grandchildren. Busy, stressed parents cannot always provide all the affirmation, patience, and unconditional love children need. Gracious and doting grandparents can fill love gaps left by harried parents and add to the love provided by nurturing, attentive ones.

Children adopt ideas about their own worth and the

trustworthiness of love from their early experience with the adults in their lives. That means grandparents who cherish and love grandchildren without condition greatly influence and help their grandchildren accept themselves, trust others, and even trust God throughout life. In *The Long Distance Grandmother*, Selma Wasserman said, "It was from my grandmother that I learned the most important things about myself—that I was loved and therefore lovable; that I was appreciated, even though I had flaws; that I was special."[2]

POMs can teach their grandchildren about God's love by offering them patience, approval, acceptance, and interest and by taking time to talk, listen, and play. Your most important function as a grandparent involves adding unconditional love to your grandchild's world.

Grandparents as Prayer Warriors

Many grandparents pray faithfully for their grandchildren. POMs who want to bless their grandchildren in this way learn how and what to pray by keeping the lines of communication open with their missionary and his or her children on the field. You can pray that God will protect your grandchildren and help them grow in character and love. Certain Scriptures you come across may offer inspiration for how to pray. Writing in *Homefront Heartbeats,* Sherrie Johnson urged POMs to pray that their grandchildren make good friends, grow to admire integrity, not feel rootless, and learn how to manage fear.[3]

Grandparents as Patriarchs and Matriarchs

The Grandparenting Great organization[4] describes two grandparenting styles, one passive and the other active. This organization derives its description from the work of David DeWitt in *The Mature Man: Becoming a Man of Impact.*

According to Grandparenting Great, some grandparents think of themselves as retired from family responsibility. They engage with family in a passive way, responding to initiatives from others for connection but seldom launching any of their own. They take a backseat role in the family, fall out of touch with current culture, and dwell in the past.

Other grandparents embrace the roles of matriarch and patriarch. They emphasize personal maturity and feel a sense of responsibility for the well-being of the family. Patriarchs and matriarchs actively seek to care for and mentor younger members of the family. They are spiritually mature, stay involved with the family, stay up to speed with cultural changes, and willingly take initiative as needed to positively influence the future.

Matriarchal and patriarchal grandparents do not direct or control; they respect the right of others to enjoy freedom within the will of God. They provide a calming influence because they know many problems can't be solved. They serve as a valuable resource to members of the younger generation because they often know the right thing to do when it conflicts with another right thing to do. Matriarchal and patriarchal grandparents do not think of themselves as on the sidelines of family life but as ministers to the family.

These grandparents sacrifice time and money to be near family, reach out to be near children and grandchildren, and prays for their loved ones. Matriarchs and patriarchs also respect the marital bond and parenting roles of their adult children. They deal with their own sin, and they hold themselves accountable to God.

Grandparents as Resources

POMs have the opportunity as grandparents to enrich their grandchildren's lives. You can introduce your grandkids to your areas of interest and expertise. You can provide funds for lessons and other educational programs and take them on exciting adventures to see and learn new things. You can share stories about other people, places, and times.

Grandchildren on the mission field love when grandparents send items they cannot get where they live, perhaps comic strips, books, DVDs, and Kool-Aid.

Grandkids feel more connected to grandma and grandpa when they have their own room and their own belongings in a grandparent's home. When grandchildren return on furlough and visit you, your home can serve as an island of stability in their sometimes mobile lives. They will appreciate the opportunity to return to the house, room, things, hugs, cooking, and friends they knew before. Laretta left the swing in her backyard even though she knew her grandchildren would be too old to enjoy it on their next furlough. "I want them to see it when they come back," she said, "to realize they will always have a place here."

POMs who want to house their missionary family during

furloughs may require more living space than their empty-nest counterparts who have family living nearby. Rose said, "We goofed when we downsized. . . . Now I see we could use more space, at least every four years when the kids are back."

Grandparents as Conduits

Grandparents can also transmit ideas, values, and culture to their grandchildren. The ideas and attitudes you teach may underscore what the parents already teach, offer an alternative perspective, or simply broaden your grandchild's awareness.

If you model Christlike qualities (grace, warmth, patience, acceptance, and care), your testimony about God's love will take on a special credibility with your grandchildren. You can also help them know God by reading (or sending) Bible stories and other special books, paying tuition to Christian camps and other programs, and participating in service projects with them either at home or during visits to the field.

When special trust develops, you have an opportunity to transmit other values that help your grandchildren develop good character. You can talk with them about integrity, loyalty, problem solving, church involvement, fiscal and civil responsibility, commitment, respect, hospitality, encouragement, affirmation, humor, and fun. As a grandparent, you may be able to get through to a grandchild when parents can't!

Your grandparent function also includes passing down a family culture. You have the opportunity to share family attitudes toward many areas of life, including ministry, music, education, extended family, physical fitness, recreation, outdoor activities, and sports. You can also share holiday traditions and attitudes toward politics, faith, worship styles, dress, and everyday matters, such as whether dinner is eaten together or individually, at a fixed time or on a flexible schedule.

Grandchildren like to learn about family history. As a grandparent, you may have the opportunity to share memories about family members and events of the past. Knowing family history helps grandkids feel connected to something larger than their immediate family. Kids who grow up on the mission field have a greater-than-normal need to feel connected and rooted to their passport culture. By passing along family history, POMs provide a context that helps children understand how the family came to its present circumstance.

Finally, POMs can help grandkids growing up on the mission field by helping them learn about their passport culture. As we discussed in chapter 8, missionary kids may not fully identify with either their host culture or their passport culture. They essentially become Third Culture Kids (TCKs) because they blend the two cultures they know and generate a culture of their own.

TCKs may struggle painfully when visiting their parents' homeland because they find themselves unversed in cultural values, speech idioms, fashion trends, and social nuances. You can help your grandchildren navigate the culture by explaining cultural differences and by sharing stories about times when you felt embarrassed or uncomfortable while visiting on the field. Providing books, magazines, DVDs, and news can help a grandchild gain cultural literacy in his family's homeland. And POMs can design experiences and trips to help grandchildren better understand the traditions, history, and values of their passport culture.

Grandparents as Role Models

By the time grandchildren arrive, most grandparents have lived long enough to sort out their values and adjust their lifestyle to reflect their values. The lifestyle you model will influence your grandchildren, for better or for worse! You can teach some of life's greatest lessons to grandchildren by modeling virtues such as trusting in God, loving life, and appreciating beauty.

Grandparenting Great

POMs can grow strong bonds with distant grandchildren by observing some fundamental grandparenting principles and by adopting a few creative ideas for building bridges. We now offer four principles for effective grandparenting that can help you build warm and positive relationships with your adult children and grandchildren. They focus on attitudes and ways of relating to others.

Respect People, Feelings, and Ideas

The children's rights movement of the 1970s made me recall my grandmother's account of having to wait as a child to eat leftover food until the adults in her family had sated their appetites and left the dinner table. Most children fare better today, but some families influenced by archaic attitudes still treat children as second-class citizens and give them little voice. But

Jesus taught us to hold, hear, and comfort children (Matthew 19:14). We need to offer children the same personal respect we afford adults.

Show concern for your grandkids' feelings and opinions. Respond to what they share with interest and empathy. Be careful not to talk down to them or make them feel like they don't know very much.

Allow grandchildren to work out their own problems instead of offering unsolicited advice. Accept differences in lifestyles, express your concerns with grace and humor, and avoid comparing or choosing favorites among your grandchildren. Also try to recognize and accept each grandchild's limitations.

Communicate Effectively

We can communicate respect through our speech. Say encouraging things like, "Do your best," instead of negative messages such as, "You should do better." You will enjoy better relationships with your grandkids and their parents if you speak for yourself by using "I" statements and avoid using directive "you" language.

Listen carefully to your grandchildren. Ask to know more about whatever interests them, their likes and dislikes. They will love it if you say things like, "I want to know about . . ." or, "Come sit close and tell me about. . . ." Find the patience to hear all the details, and even if you feel lonely, avoid talking too much about yourself or repeating the same stories.

Your youthful grandchildren will likely say and do things now and then that feel hurtful. When this happens, avoid defensive responses that shut down conversation and create emotional distance. Simply state what you think or feel, and look for ways to ease a difficult situation.

Visit and Share Activities

Visits and shared activities greatly enhance the grandparent/ grandchild bond. While electronic connections help immensely during times of separation, they cannot offer the same warmth that comes with personal contact. Rose said, "Nothing takes the place of being together." Jan commented on the unique quality of connection that comes only during personal visits: "On our first visit . . . Jake, who was seven, clung to my hand, looked and looked at me for several days, as if to fix me in his memory."

Experienced POMs tell us the gains that come from personal visits with family on the mission field justify all the time, money, and effort such visits cost. Not all POMs can travel to the mission field, but those who do visit find it very worthwhile. Jim said, "One of the best ways to stay connected is to visit as often as possible; our grandkids know we care enough to become involved in their lives overseas."

Playing together can help POMs build bonds and create memories that will keep your relationship vital through times of separation. Positive feelings come rushing back when you or your grandchild says, "Remember when we . . . ."

Have a Positive Attitude and Offer Choices

As a grandparent, you may find yourself more relaxed and

more inclined to "stop and smell the roses" than your grandchild's busy and stressed parents. If so, recognize that you have an opportunity to help your grandchild develop a sense of wonderment and fun about life. You can help build your grandchildren's confidence by remaining relaxed and nondirective and by encouraging them to explore the world and make choices for themselves.

Proven Ways to Stay Close across the Miles

Perhaps you identify with Gaylen, who wrote, "I'm looking for creative ways to participate in my grandson's life over multiple time zones and thousands of miles." We asked POMs to tell us how they stay connected with grandchildren on the field. These tested ideas are sure to help you and your grandchildren connect as well.

Use the Mail

"All kids love mail," wrote Lori, a missionary, "but MKs especially know the value of mail." Even though today's technology makes instant communication possible, a card or letter from grandma or grandpa with a packet of Kool-Aid, sticks of gum, or funny jokes slipped inside make "snail mail" from grandparents "wonderful and greatly anticipated," she wrote.

Letters from Grandma. Each year Rose gives her grandchildren an album filled with clear page protectors. Throughout the year she sends letters and photos about experiences she shared with that child. "I record where we went, what we did and said, my grandchild's reactions and expressions, my prayers for him or her . . . it creates an enduring connection," she said.

Grandma's Book-of-the-Month Club. Rose also created the Grandma's Book-of-the-Month Club, sending a different book each month. "These are especially appreciated in regions where books in English are hard to find," she said.

Grandkids' Mail-of-the-Month Club. For Christmas, Rose's grandchildren gave her a binder with clear page protectors and coupons good for mail from the grandchildren each month for a year.

Birthday in a Box. Lori, a missionary, reported that each year her parents sent her kids a "birthday in a box"—plates, hats, streamers, balloons, a box of favorite cereal for a special birthday breakfast, and often a new video to be enjoyed at the birthday party. "My kids knew they were treasured by two very special people who loved them *so* much," said Lori.

Magazines and Newspapers. Purchase two subscriptions to a favorite children's or teen magazine, one for you and one for your grandchild. If direct international mailing isn't possible, have both subscriptions sent to your home and forward one overseas in a flat-rate international mailing envelope. Write or talk to your grandchild about each issue.

Ken, with grandkids ages ten and twelve, wrote, "For the last four years I've sent a package every Monday morning containing the comics from the past week's newspapers." He includes current issues of magazines too. The cost to send a Priority Mail International Flat Rate envelope to most countries is currently $11.00. "It is worth every penny," Ken said.

Send a coloring book to your grandchild and ask that some completed pictures be mailed to you. Put them on your fridge, take a picture, and send the photo to your grandchild.

Use Your Camera and Computer

Computers and cameras can be used in more than the obvious ways. Here are more ideas from creative POMs who are staying connected to grandkids far away.

Personalized Puzzles. Create crossword and word-search puzzles using words your grandchild knows, words in Scripture they will look up, names of people they know or places they've been, or words from their hobbies and interests. Internet websites make it easy to create personalized word-search and crossword puzzles. Print out the puzzles to send in a card or letter or try e-mailing them. Check out these sites:

www.puzzles.ca/wordsearch.html

www.puzzlemaker.discoveryeducation.com

Get Creative with Digital Photos. Several POMs told of creating cards for playing Memory. Carol wrote:

Use twenty-six photos of family members

and life at home and/or on the mission field. Have two of every photo printed wallet size and laminate them to use for playing Memory. Small, color-coded numbers and symbols in corners also make the cards useable in standard card games. (In case you've never played Memory, all cards go face down in rows on the table. The first player lifts two random cards to see if they match. If they do, that player collects the cards and takes another turn. If the cards do not match, play passes to the next person. When all the cards have been matched, the person with the most matches wins.)

Personalized calendars make great gifts. Use the services of a photo store or online photo site to make calendars for your grandchildren that feature pictures of you or of you and the grandchildren together.

Provide your grandchildren with disposable cameras; then ask them to take crazy pictures of themselves and send the camera back to you. Or give them a digital camera; there are some children's versions available now. Ask for the photos to be e-mailed or posted on a family blog or photo site.

Take pictures of yourself at work, at home, at church, and engaged in hobbies and ministry activities. Photos like these help grandchildren feel part of their grandparents' lives.

Before Laura and her family returned home for a family wedding, her mother sent photos of all extended family members, even the dogs, with names at the bottom of each picture. She attached small magnets to the back of each picture and included a small magnetic board—all in a resealable plastic bag. On the long flight home, wrote Laura, "It was a real help [to my three-year-old] and even my husband to learn names of family that we rarely see, and it even helped me to mentally switch gears as I thought of meeting them."

Cindy's daughter put pictures of family members in a plastic photo album designed for babies (often available in stores that sell children's books). "Our granddaughter can play with [it]," Cindy said. "She looks at it and they talk about who each person is."

"Ask [your missionary] to show pictures of you to your young grandchildren while they open packages sent from you or talk with you on the phone," suggested one POM. "This helps them connect the gifts and voice with your face."

Sandy told this heartwarming story of the effect of a single photo: "Our grandchild was born during our children's overseas missionary service. We saw him shortly after birth. Our children put a picture of us in a plastic frame and had it on a table where he could reach it. He was permitted to handle the picture. When we went to visit when he was two years old, he gave us a big spontaneous smile when he saw us through the glass at the airport."

Books and Videos. Several POMs recommended reading picture books aloud on an audiotape, videotape, or DVD, using a bell to signal when it's time to turn the page, and then sending the recording and book to grandchildren on the mission field. "Grandkids will listen to these over and over again," one missionary observed, "even into their teen years, because they love to hear the voices of the grandparents they love."

Jeanne and her husband, Johnny, wrote about the "Grandpa's Camp" videos they create and send to their grandchildren. Johnny made up a song that starts every video; then he introduces the theme, reads a book, shares a snack (sent with the video), and goes "on location" or gives a demonstration. His subjects so far have included camping, photography (at the Grand Canyon), music (the church orchestra), a sick day, Christmas, Fourth of July, and Bible stories. Sometimes the grandchildren's cousins are included too!

Building Bridges

Separation from grandchildren causes real pain for POMs. "It's a difficult way to live," said Rhonda. Janice found it the hardest part of being a POM. Dawn called it "the pits." Bill and Mary noted that saying good-bye has not gotten easier with practice. Despite the pain, however, we want to urge hurting grandparents to build bridges as well as to grieve. POMs face both pain and choice. Even though you hurt, you still must choose between sinking into sad helplessness and grandparenting great across the miles!

It takes extra dedication to grandparent well over long distances, but you can succeed if you catch the vision and recognize your potential to bless distant grandchildren and enjoy loving relationships. Simply learn the relevant skills and then spend the time, energy, and money it takes to connect well.

I want to close this chapter with a story shared by Frieda,

a POM grandma who knew she could make a positive difference in the lives of her distant grandkids. Frieda cared enough about her connection to those kids to buy and learn how to use a webcam.

One day, Frieda's missionary daughter had to go to the hospital for surgery, causing her three young children to be left with a babysitter all day until their daddy came home from the hospital. When Frieda's son-in-law called over the Internet to say the surgery had gone well, Frieda could see a very sad look on the face of her six-year-old granddaughter, Jemma:

> When I asked Jemma what was the matter, big tears started rolling down her cheeks. She said, "I haven't seen Mommy all day and she won't be coming home tonight." That just broke my heart. . . . As a grandma one would so much like to be there to stay with the children at a time like this. I immediately reached for a storybook, one that we enjoyed together when they were here. I held it up to the webcam and asked Jemma if she could see the book and which one it was. She was able to see it and told me the title. I asked her if she would like me to read it to her and she was pleased about that. The other two children (eight and four) also came to listen.
>
> I read the whole book to them, showing them all the pictures that they could see quite easily. We chatted about the story in between pages, just like we always did when they were here. It was awesome.

My heart soared as I sensed that feeling of closeness once again. . . . We had such a great time, and Jemma was able to get past her feelings of sadness. . . . I had to stop and marvel that in spite of the fact that we are living two continents apart, we were able to have such a great time together.

Frieda's efforts to be a connected grandma were richly rewarded. Her story serves as an encouraging reminder that while no grandparent wants to be separated from grandchildren, loved ones can be close even when they live far apart.

HAPPY HOLIDAYS?

Coping with Holiday Stress

Now Mark and I are wondering what we'll do for
Christmas this year.

—a POM mom

We all know the holidays bring joy, right?

Each of us can sing from memory the Thanksgiving hymns and Christmas carols that articulate our heart's gladness when Thanksgiving and Christmas roll around. Later, Easter brings the hustle-bustle of shopping for new clothes and planning special family dinners. Next come summer family reunions. Holidays afford so many opportunities for fun!

Yet as a POM with family on the mission field, your heart may resonate more with Elvis's "Blue Christmas." One POM mom honestly admitted, "I really struggle with the holidays and birthdays. Holidays are the worst. Christmas once was my favorite but now I dread it every year. Actually I hate it. We've spent Christmases alone and it's no fun. I'm trying to avoid the holidays but that's hard because we all know they go on for months!" Despite all the festivities and appearances of gladness, many POMs simply do not feel gloriously happy through the holiday season and on other special dates.

The holidays purport to help us celebrate God's blessings, our hope in Jesus Christ, and the freedom we enjoy. However, we can and should celebrate these things every day. Holidays become special mainly because family members who normally stay busy and live apart pause and come together to celebrate shared love, and in families of faith, shared hope.

POMs may find it hard to celebrate Thanksgiving, Christmas, Easter, birthdays, and other family occasions cheerfully because, like everyone else, they'd prefer to have their loved ones around at these times. Their hearts do not resonate when radios and store speakers blare about hearts glowing because loved ones are near. Instead, POMs separated from loved ones often find their grief intensifies during holiday seasons when the time comes for traditional family gatherings.

Holiday Grinches That Steal Joy

As a POM, you may feel especially vulnerable to emotional, mental, and physical disturbances during holiday and other special seasons. The "holiday blues" involve feelings of discouragement and loss of courage about life—they hurt! I (Cheryl) want to encourage you to reduce your risk of suffering by carefully avoiding certain pitfalls that contribute to this experience.

Exhaustion

The bar of cultural standards and expectations seems to rise every year in many areas of life, including the way we observe holidays. My father recalled with warm feelings the simple Christmas celebrations his family shared in their home above the family store during the 1920s. Household decorations included only holly hung over the door and a small tree in the corner, decorated with homemade ornaments and candles lit briefly on Christmas Eve. Dad and his siblings felt blessed to find oranges (a treat during Midwestern winters) stuffed in their stockings and a simple gift or two under the tree. Today, barring extreme poverty, we might suspect emotional depression in our parents if they "under decorated," and we might disapprove if they provided so little for their children at Christmas.

Our present social environment makes it hard for us to keep Christmas simple. Television stations celebrate the most extravagant (sometimes ridiculous) yard displays. Stores push must-have decorations to transform our homes into festive wonderlands. Friends invite each other in to enjoy (or compare) decorative prowess (no pressure here!). Schools, churches, companies, and clubs organize parties that require special holiday clothes and pressure us to dazzle. (Ladies, make your salon appointments early to beat the holiday rush!) Most gatherings require that we bring sweet delicacies and gifts to share (homemade and handmade preferred—hope you have time). We overspend and take on debt to finance our holiday frenzy. We exhaust ourselves trying to ensure our holiday observance rises to meet the latest standard!

Until we deliberately simplify holiday celebrations, most of us will continue to feel stressed, pressed, and exhausted through Christmas and other special occasions. We will stay up late doing unnecessary things (that feel necessary) and lie awake recounting all we have to do in the holiday spirit of stress, not peace! We may fail to eat right, exercise, or nourish ourselves spiritually and feel our holiday spirit wane as the holiday blues emerge.

Disappointed Childhood Fantasies

The fairy tales we enjoyed as children prompted us to fantasize and nurture naive hopes for a happily-ever-after life of contentment, security, and perfect circumstances. While God does offer us complete contentment and security, He doesn't provide them through perfect circumstances, nor does He promise us happiness in this life. To the contrary, Scripture promises us trouble in this world (Matthew 6:34), especially if we're married (1 Corinthians 7:28).

We generally understand this reality by the time we reach adulthood. Still, the holidays have a way of rousing childhood hopes and dreams from forgotten places in our hearts. Reflecting on resurrected dreams that did not come true can make us feel sad. You might feel sad during the holidays because your missionary lives far away, because your marriage does not meet fairy-tale standards, because your home does not look like a castle or the brutal mirror tells you to forget "fairest of them all." Disappointed dreams contribute to our holiday blues.

Family Tensions

The holidays sometimes leave family relationships feeling strained. Minor tensions can arise when family members find that living together in intense closeness is less romantic than they anticipated. Irritability develops around issues such as room temperature, promptness to dinner and other engagements, consideration for others while using a bathroom, and standards for cell phone use and otherwise holding private conversations in the presence of others.

Tensions that are more serious result when families try to celebrate the holidays together without first resolving interpersonal problems simmering beneath the surface. Many POMs live in family situations where marriage issues, sibling rivalries, parent/child problems, and parent/in-law problems fester unresolved.

Expectations of Holiday Cheer

Music, shining lights, enchanting decorations, romantic movies, and special meals all set the stage for birthday and holiday cheer. We only need to supply a personal burst of happiness. Oddly enough, while feeling so-so or even a little blue seems perfectly acceptable on an everyday basis, such feelings seem terribly out of place on special days when we expect happiness to soar. We expect the holidays and special family occasions to provide an emotional high, and we feel especially disappointed when separation from family, exhaustion, unfulfilled dreams, and unresolved family tensions dampen our mood.

We sometimes erroneously assume everyone else feels happy amid the holiday bustle and blame ourselves for feeling down or blame others for stealing our joy. Our culture conditions us to expect happiness during the holidays, making normal life problems (that don't magically disappear on command) seem particularly hard to accept on festive occasions.

Loss

We live in an increasingly mobile society that causes increasing numbers of us to live without the comfort of having loved ones immediately near. We want and hope to see our family members on holidays and birthdays. While all families must eventually grieve during the holidays due to the death of a loved one, most families who live apart still live close enough to make holiday gatherings feasible—unless part of the family lives halfway around the world serving as a missionary!

As a POM, you may grieve through the holidays over both bereavement and separation from your family on the mission field. Your may feel stinging pain as you conjure up special memories of childhood birthday parties and Christmas dinners shared in the past. Empty seats at the family table may cause whatever celebration you organize to feel strangely unfulfilling. Many POMs experience a kind of stunned disbelief during the first year of separation and find the second equally painful because it drives home the permanency of the unwanted separation.

Reclaiming Holiday Joy

While many POMs experience the holidays as sad and difficult, others have found ways to enjoy special days, even when their missionary is away. Coping with separation during the holidays may be hardest in the beginning. Gradually, however, you can develop the capacity to find positive meaning in your circumstances and make choices that enable you to experience holiday joy.

Making Positive Meaning

We choose how we think about circumstances and the things that happen to us; we can assign very different meanings to a single event or set of circumstances. And how we think influences how we feel.

For example, you'll feel sad about your child's decision to become a missionary if you think in terms of abandonment, if you assume he or she does not care about family relationships, or if you hold fast to the conviction that families *should* be together for the holidays. While such thoughts may naturally occur as you adjust to being a POM, they leave you feeling blue and cheated.

You will feel better if you look for positive ways to make your circumstances meaningful. Marina shared how she managed to think positively about being separated from her family during the Christmas season:

This Christmas our son is going on a short-term mission trip to South America, our oldest daughter is on a mission field in Asia, and our other daughter whose husband is in the ministry will want to stay at home to serve their church and be with their new baby. I would not think of imposing on them, or expecting them to travel the two thousand miles to our home in the middle of winter! Likewise, our daughter in Asia will only get Christmas Day off, and they have their semester finals shortly after the holidays. It's not a good time to travel to see them!

We are jumping at the chance to not be bound to our kids during the holidays. It was important to us as a newlywed couple, and then as parents, to establish family traditions in our home. We feel it is right to free our kids and allow them to start their own family traditions, and for them not to have to include driving or flying to our house!

Marina does not think of herself as unloved and abandoned but as a mother giving the gift of freedom to her adult children who have pressures and needs of their own. Her positive way of making her circumstances meaningful will help Marina feel better through Christmas.

Positive Choices

In addition to thinking about circumstances in positive ways, POMs can cope better with the holidays if they intentionally choose to make the holidays better. We think your holidays will go better if you choose to take the following steps.

Plan Ahead to Avoid Exhaustion. The whirlwind of expectations and activities that surround the holidays can leave us feeling spent. Exhaustion challenges our immune system and our ability to think rationally, and it places us at risk for emotional disturbances like sadness, anxiety, and irritability. POMs struggling with sadness and grief can reduce their risk of stress overload by planning ahead to keep holiday observances relatively simple.

Acknowledge Your Grief. You may naturally grieve during the holidays because of family separations or other life disappointments. You may need to accept that some lifelong dreams will not be realized and acknowledge that loss. Perhaps you always dreamed of your missionary and grandchildren living nearby, but now you recognize that won't happen. You may have expected your health or a loved one's health to hold up better, but now you face the unpleasant realities of illness or even bereavement. It can help to set aside time to experience such pain, to talk to God and safe others about it, and to express your pain through outlets such as journaling.

Let Go of "Oughts." Try not to torture yourself by criticizing your feelings, believing that you should feel differently than you do. If you feel sad about your separation from loved ones or because of other life disappointments, accept your feelings as a normal reaction to loss.

Arrange for Personal Support. POMs may feel a need for extra care and support through the holiday season and on other special days. Why not schedule some personal downtime, arrange to be with a close friend who listens without judging, and spend some extra time talking with God? Plan a new kind of holiday activity, and invite others to join you.

Address Family Issues Before the Holidays. We can reduce unwanted holiday tensions within our families by taking time to address problems before the holidays arrive. Identify any unresolved problems that simmer below the surface in your family. Then meet with the involved family members to resolve the problems before the family celebration.

For example, if you find your husband is overcommitted to work, don't wait until the holidays begin, company arrives, and everyone feels tired, tense, and emotional to tell him how it feels. Or, if you think your wife gives more attention to the kids than to you, don't wait until the festivities begin to tell her or sulk through them in withdrawn silence, nursing your resentment. If whatever adult children you have present seem competitive, tell them before the holidays that you'd like them to offer more support to one another during the family celebration this year.

Clarify Holiday Expectations with Family in Advance. Expectations for the holidays tend to run high and come packed with emotion. POMs can reduce the incidences of family tensions, conflicts, misunderstandings, surprises, and disappointments by communicating plans and needs with family early. It helps when we communicate our preferences and desires without burdening others with expectations.

We recommend two steps. First, find out what every family member would like to do and can do; second, based on that information, generate a holiday plan that everyone can agree to. Ideally, plans for Thanksgiving and Christmas should take shape by late October. Who will go where? When? What kind of gift exchange will work best for everyone?

Think on What's Good. Try making a list of all the blessings you enjoy as a result of being a POM. The list might surprise you. You may have met other POMs and made new friends, acquired a broader worldview, learned more about another country and missions in general, learned about yourself, drawn closer to God as a result of your struggle, and have some upcoming opportunities for travel. Also, to remind yourself that God remains present with you despite the losses you've suffered, recount all the unrelated good things God has done in your life since you became a POM.

Connect with Other POMs. As always, we encourage you to connect with other POMs. Get on a newsletter list, find or start a POM group, attend conventions, talk with leaders and other knowledgeable people in your own church. Stay in contact with other POMs you know at least once a week through the holiday season and other difficult times. If possible, organize your own holiday POM get-together.

Invent New Ways to Celebrate with Your Missionary.
With a little creativity you can find ways to celebrate with your
loved ones on the mission field. Try reading special stories to
your grandchildren on tape. Buy two copies of a holiday movie,
send one overseas, and talk about it together after everyone has
watched it. Create an e-mail journal of your holiday preparations
and activities. Open gifts while on the phone or webcam, and
share digital photos. Invite your missionary's closest friends to
share your celebration and serve some international dishes from
his or her host country.

Change Traditions. Doing things differently may ease
the pain of family separation. If you've always done *X* for
Thanksgiving, Christmas, or a special birthday, try doing *Y* this
year. Instead of limiting Thanksgiving or Christmas dinner to
immediate family members, include friends or others.

Including new people in your holiday celebrations will fill
the chairs that otherwise seem so empty, and you might find
your new guests appreciative, gracious, interesting, and worth
knowing better. If you've always stayed home for Christmas, why
not try getting out of the house or even out of town this year?
That way, even if the house is quiet, you won't be there to notice!
Marina has a can-do attitude about Christmas without kids:

> We are considering our options about how to
> celebrate Christmas now that we are POMs. We
> jokingly mentioned holiday cruises from here on
> out, but realize that it would be cost prohibitive if
> we ever want to go Asia to visit on the field. Mark's

mom has bought a home in Florida, and it would be a nice treat to visit there. We can stay home and invite others in—reaching out to foreign students or young families who do not have a place to be for the holidays. We may serve at a homeless shelter on Christmas Day or deliver Meals on Wheels. It will be interesting to see how the holiday will play out over the next few years. We will be content anywhere God would open the doors.

Visit Your Missionary. Some POMs make a tradition of visiting their missionary over Christmas. Admittedly, work schedules and financial limitations can preclude this option, but when it is possible, it can be fun. Ken wrote:

> Susan and I have always been close, and when I visited her in the summer of 2004 we talked about me coming back for Christmas. I had retired and we both said, "Why not?" So I did and was very glad since I got to go to all the kids' programs, church services, celebrations on the town square, and the like. It makes two-plus weeks seem like a very good, fulfilling time with them. I've spent the last three Christmases there.

Be Gentle and Proactive

If you find yourself dreading birthdays and holidays because your family lives so far away, please be gentle with yourself and accept that you have perfectly understandable reasons for your struggle. However, please recognize that if you can manage to find positive meaning in your circumstances and take proactive steps to enhance your holiday experience, you can do well through special-occasion days—despite separation from loved ones.

Even if separation means your holidays won't be, as the song says, "the most wonderful time of the year," you can choose to make them very, very good.

HIGH-TECH AND NO-TECH WAYS TO STAY CLOSE

12

Connecting through Mail and Media

*I praise God for the way we can communicate
now. I just received pictures via the Internet of the
granddaughters in an African wedding.*

—a POM dad

How do you connect with your missionary halfway or more around the world? For this chapter I (Diane) have rounded up tips that worked for me and my family as well as a host of ideas straight from other POMs.

Not every idea here will work for every situation. If your missionary lives in a region where a high measure of security is necessary or where phone and Internet access are miles away, adapting will be necessary. Don't let that stop you from doing everything that *is* possible in your situation to stay connected with your missionary.

Mail and Shipping

Even with e-mail and other modern ways to stay in touch, sometimes you want to send something handwritten, small gifts, or items your missionary has requested.

Options for Getting It There

Stock up on cards for birthdays and holidays as well as "thinking of you" and encouragement cards. Check with your post office about postage and delivery times, and send cards well in advance so they arrive on time.

If you live in the United States, the best mailing rates are likely the Priority Mail International Flat Rate envelope and box. The flat-rate envelope is 9.5 by 12.5 inches and may contain personal correspondence as well as other items, up to the 4-pound weight limit. The envelope must enclose the items with the envelope flap in its normal position, although tape to reinforce the closure is allowed. At the beginning of 2008, the cost to send a flat-rate Priority Mail International envelope to Canada or Mexico was $9.00; to all other countries the cost was $11.00.

The maximum weight for the flat-rate box is 20 pounds or the limit set by the country you are sending to, whichever is less. "Current and personal" correspondence is not allowed in a flat-rate box. The rate to Canada and Mexico at the beginning of 2008 was $23.00, $37.00 to all other countries.

Services such as FedEx and DHL are the best options for fast shipping, but they're also the most expensive.

Some Internet shopping services such as amazon.com offer international shipping. This can save you time but most likely will not save you money. Be sure to read all the shipping information posted on the website. Never send Christian materials to missionaries (or nationals) in closed countries. If your missionary works in a closed country, you must be vigilant never to send (or say or write) anything that might endanger your missionary or the nationals with whom he has contact. See the section "Closed-Country Guidelines" a little later in this chapter.

Tips for Packing and Sending Packages

You may be able to send items to your missionary with someone who is traveling to the area where your missionary lives. Ask members of your church or other organizations to let you know if their travel plans will take them near your missionary. "If a person stays alert," wrote Jim, "you will hear of someone making the trip [to your missionary's field]. For instance, I am sending one granddaughter's birthday gift with a single guy from our church who is going over to work with them for a year. Then, our son-in-law's parents are going over at Christmas, so I will send a box to them to take for us."

Lynn, a POM and former missionary, cautioned POMs to be careful about the kinds of items packed in the same box: "Mom learned the hard way not to ship perfume-y things in with boxed food items," she said. "We had to tell her we just couldn't eat the Zest-flavored strawberry Jell-O."

Getting Technical

Connecting regularly with your missionary by phone, e-mail, or Internet lends a sense of normalcy to your relationship. If you use the latest technologies at your place of employment, you may already know the basics of international calling and Internet use. If not, don't hesitate to ask someone to help you learn, or take a computer class! "Modern technology is truly wonderful," wrote Frieda, a POM, "and I encourage any parents or grandparents who are able to access this type of communication to do so. It is so wonderful and truly helps ease the pain of separation."

Phone Options

If phones are accessible where your missionary lives, stay in touch by phone. "Even when our grandbaby was only weeks old," said Cindy, "I always asked to talk with her (if she was awake). My daughter would put the phone up to her ear so that she could hear my voice. I felt connected even if she wouldn't remember. . . . She is now sixteen months old and actually talks to us on the phone each week. It is so fun to hear her progress in learning new words."

My husband and I called our daughter and son-in-law once or twice a month for long conversations. Other POMs phone their missionary more often. "We called weekly at roughly the same time each week," said Sandy. "Our children have been asked if they felt smothered by our phone calls. They indicated that the calls were their lifeline!"

It may be much cheaper for you to call your missionary than for your missionary to call you. Shop around for the best phone and rate options. "To get the cost down to the bare bones, you need good information, a willingness to try new things, and a commitment to try new things," wrote the "Everyday Cheapskate," Mary Hunt.[1]

Many companies offer international calling cards. Be sure to compare calling card rates for the country you will be calling. Our family enjoyed using a card from Nobelcom.com (www.nobelcom.com), which allowed us to talk four hours for just twenty dollars. Hunt recommends PennyTalk (www.pennytalk.com). With both of these companies, you set up an account on at the company website and add money to your account with a credit card. Charges for calls are then deducted from your account, and you can set your account to recharge automatically so you're never without calling time. Many plans allow you to make calls to or from cell phones as well as landline phones. One POM wrote, "We were pleasantly surprised to find that in Uganda, one only pays for cell phone calls made and not cell phone calls received. That means we can talk to [our sons] pretty reasonably."

Voice-over-Internet technology, also known as VoIP, lets you call anywhere in the world over the Internet. Because most plans charge per month, not per minute, and assign a local number to the destination you are calling, the cost savings can be great. You connect to a VoIP network using a VoIP telephone, a normal telephone with a VoIP adapter, or a computer with speakers and a microphone. Probably the best-known VoIP company, and one of the first, is Vonage (www.vonage.com).

Skype is a free Internet calling program that offers video calls (www.skype.com). If both you and your missionary have high-speed cable connections, download the software, add a microphone and speakers to your computer systems, and you're set.

Other Internet Options

E-mail and instant messaging are basic to communicating over the Internet. E-mail allows you to send "letters" electronically, hence the name. Instant-messaging programs allow you to *chat* (write messages) with your missionary in *real time* (as opposed to sending an e-mail and waiting for a reply).

E-mail allows you to send personalized *e-cards* to your missionary and grandchildren on special occasions or for no reason at all, free or for a small fee. Check out the collections of e-cards offered by Hallmark (www.hallmark.com) and Blue Mountain (www.bluemountain.com).

The Internet is great for sharing digital photos and videos. Blogs (like a journal, but online) and social-networking sites such as Facebook provide a way for families to post news, photos, and videos. If your missionary establishes a blog or a Facebook page, be sure to learn how to access it. Grandparents especially enjoy seeing photos, photo slide shows, and videos of their grandchildren—and you can watch them again whenever you want to! "Our son-in-law sends us a few digital pictures via e-mail each Sunday night," said Cindy. "We look forward to seeing them first thing on Monday mornings. He also sends short video clips occasionally. We have watched her learn how to smile, walk, and talk."

Adding a webcam to your computer and using a video-calling program such as Skype or MSN Messenger allows POMs and missionaries to connect in so many wonderful ways. You'll enjoy seeing one another while you talk, and it's free! Frieda wrote, "While we are chatting, our son-in-law often sends us e-mails with pictures he has taken with his digital camera. While we are watching our grandchildren open their birthday presents, he takes pictures of them and sends them to us. (They are clearer than what we are able to see with the webcam.) Other times he has sent us e-mail pictures of various places they have visited and then we can discuss them with him as we look at them. It is just like sitting together and looking at a photo album."

Bonnie, a POM, said, "We usually 'meet' very early on Saturday mornings. We don't know how we could endure the separation if it weren't for video chat! I think [our son] would say the same thing. Our favorite memory is when there was a parade of mountain people and animals going by under his balcony. He was able to attach his camcorder to his computer, go out on the balcony, and we were able to watch the parade with him. It was so cool!"

Communication Challenges

If you are able to use e-mail and the Internet to connect with your missionary, consider these challenges and work with your missionary to find the best ways to handle them.

Time Busters

If you have an instant-messaging program or a video-calling program on your computer, when you're online you can see those on your contact list who are also online or when they sign on. I found it fun to see the message "Sheila has just signed on" appear in the corner of my computer screen, but rarely did I follow up to chat with her, especially in her early years on the field. Why? Because I knew she needed to be present where she was, and if she wanted to contact me at that particular time, she would.

Doug, a missionary, said, "We want to acknowledge our families' sacrifice but we want to 'be here' when we are here, and this impacts communication in general and e-mail in particular. Communication is different over here. It is hot and e-mail is slow; it's not fun to sit and type. Heidi's sibs wanted to Skype, but we said no."

Technology can be both a blessing and a curse, and I chose not to be part of the curse. Instead, when I saw that Sheila was online at the same time I was, I envisioned her sitting in her apartment at her computer, and I enjoyed knowing where she was and what she was doing at that moment. Later on, it became more common for us to use instant messaging or video calling for short conversations to exchange information or to just say hello. Her family's ministry was established, and we all had adjusted to sharing life on two continents.

Concealing Difficulties

Sometimes POMs and missionaries wonder how much they

should share about the difficulties they're experiencing. Neither wants to worry the other unnecessarily. Susan, who has been both a missionary and a POM, wrote: "When some rough spot comes along, whether a health issue, or a bump in team member relationships, or a family member temporarily acting inappropriately, share these hardships with one another. We learned the hard way. We didn't want to be told after the fact that a loved one was having a serious surgery. We wanted to pray through it with the rest of the family. (If there are things to rejoice about, share those too.) Even though it may hurt at the time, it's better to feel a part of family life."

Another missionary echoed Susan's thoughts when she wrote:

> My own parents kept the seriousness of my mother's illness from me for a couple years. In my heart I knew there was something seriously wrong. I would hear something in my father's voice when he was on the phone, but he wouldn't admit anything. When I got back home and discovered how very ill she was, I was so angry with them for withholding this information. I felt like I had been excluded from the only thing I could have done, and that was praying for her. It was only after her death that I learned the reason my father wouldn't say anything—Mom had made him promise not to tell me. She didn't want me to worry, and she knew I couldn't go home.

Closed-Country Guidelines

If your missionary lives in a country where evangelizing is illegal, he or she gives up the right to privacy in correspondence. This may also apply to e-mails and phone conversations. Team Expansion, a sending agency, provides the following guidelines for corresponding with missionaries in closed countries. Some of these may be appropriate as well if your missionary lives in a restricted-access country:

- Don't criticize the government in any way.
- Don't mention missions, missionary activity, evangelism, witnessing, Bible distributions, the national church, support raising, etc.
- Don't send missionary prayer letters, tracts, church bulletins, missions magazines, etc.
- Don't send letters on church stationery or send support information. . . . Any sermon tapes mailed should be labeled only with the speaker's first and last name, for example, Sam Smith, not Rev. Sam Smith.
- Don't mention by name any national friends of the missionary or in any way identify national people who might be interested in Christianity.
- Limit your use of Christian language to talking about your own spiritual life and growth. You may be able to quote Scripture and to tell them that you are praying for them. Just remember, moderation is the key.
- Do write letters to the missionary. It will be cherished and bring needed encouragement. Even if you can't say

everything you would like to say, please do write. It is a good idea to tape letters closed after sealing them.[2]

Prayer by the Light of the Moon

Even if no other communication options are available to us, we can stay connected as a family if we pray for one another. Ask your missionary how you can pray for him or her, for his or her spouse, and for your grandchildren, and be faithful to pray for them.

"I told my two grandchildren about the G'ma and Pappa Moon," wrote Deb. "Every time the full moon is in the sky we think about each other and remember each other in prayer, because the moon is not only looking down on them but the same moon is looking down on G'ma and Pappa."

Rita, a veteran POM, reported, "I must say that having one of our children working on the other side of the globe has certainly enhanced our prayer life. We do a lot of that and God gets us through it all. . . . God is good."

Another POM testified to the connection POMs and their missionaries have through our good God:

It was during the days before the satellite phone and frequent e-mail that I learned that even when the possibilities for communication were at a minimum, we had a connection through God. Once I dreamed that my son was crying. The dream was so upsetting to me that I cried through church the next day. Feeling silly, I sent an e-mail to him, telling about my dream and my need to hear some reassurance from him. In a few days, I got a phone call, and my son said, "Mom, you dreamed I was crying because I was crying." He told me they had finally gotten to a place where they could watch the family video footage we had mailed them. The video was taken on the occasion of the birth of a new niece. They had watched it and wept at all they were missing not being with the family. That incident taught me that beyond any means of human communication, God himself connects us, and for that I am thankful.

THE WORLD IS MY NEIGHBORHOOD

13

Travel to the Field

Something that helped . . . was buying a globe and making a conscious effort to call the whole world our neighborhood. The other thing that has helped was to visit our missionary kids in the field. By doing that we have become a part of the mission.

—a POM mom

If you get only one thing out of this chapter, I (Diane) hope it will be this: a determination to make the trip to visit your missionary on the field. Despite whatever difficulties the trip might involve, it will be worth it not only for you but also for your missionary. Of course, some POMs face circumstances such as health issues that make international travel impossible, or their missionary does highly secretive work in a closed country, making a visit from parents dangerous and unwise. But if you're able to go, what are you waiting for?

Why Go?

Our daughter and son-in-law had been on the field for seven months when my husband and I made our first trip to visit them. Other than short jaunts into Mexico and Canada, this was my husband's first trip out of the country. I had made just one trip, a business trip, to Italy two years earlier (but I took Sheila with me as my "travel guide" because she had traveled internationally several times before). So my husband and I felt like we were wearing newbie buttons as we boarded our plane in Cincinnati in early spring. But we wouldn't have missed that trip or our second visit four years later for anything. Based on our experiences and the experiences of others, here are four big benefits of traveling to the field to visit your missionary.

Peace of Mind

By the time we drove to the apartment building where Sheila and Scoggins lived, we'd been traveling for nearly twenty-four hours. I was tired and had felt out of place ever since we walked into the Croatia Airlines section of the Amsterdam airport. Conversations now were in a language we had never heard before. The demeanor of the travelers around us was different too; everyone sat and spoke quietly. In Zagreb, where we landed, the airport buildings were old and small; we deplaned outside and were bussed into the terminal. Still, all was quiet. Slowly we made our way through customs, answering questions put to us in hard-to-understand English.

Finally, we had our bags—and there were Sheila and Scoggins, waving to us and then hugging us! For a few minutes things seemed normal again. Then we all scrunched into the small borrowed car and began the two-and-a-half-hour drive to their city, looking out the window at village homes surrounded by goats and chickens and at burned-out homes pockmarked by bullets.

Their city, with its economy ruined by war just a few years earlier, seemed to sleep in a foggy, tired haze. Scoggins pulled into a gravel parking lot and parked the car. As we climbed out, I took in the lawn of dirt and weeds and the graffiti written all over the building's lower level. I remember thinking, *This is where they LIVE?* We climbed the dusty cement stairwell to their apartment on the fifth floor. Sheila opened the door, and we stepped into a sparkling, comfortable apartment.

It was the first of many times I would be encouraged to see that my daughter was thriving and that she and her husband were happy with the life they were discovering for God in this "strange" place.

On that trip to Bosnia, we explored the little grocery store on the first floor of the kids' apartment building, with its beautiful daily offerings of fresh produce, meats, and breads. We also shopped at the two larger grocery stores in town, one reminiscent of the warehouse-style stores where we live and the other an extensive outdoor market. As we sat in cafés, drinking cappuccino with Sheila and Scoggins' language teacher and Shelia's band mates, we enjoyed the relational, relaxed aspect of the culture. We walked and shopped along the walking street, amazed at the number of young people who called out to our daughter and son-in-law and stopped to talk with them in Serbo-Croatian!

We ate in the city's only Mexican and Chinese restaurants and in the restaurant of a thousand-year-old castle. We sat in a club where our daughter's band was performing, we worshiped with the mission team in the home of one of the team families, and we picnicked on a steep, grassy hillside. We watched the local basketball team play and met our son-in-law's friend on the team. We visited the Orthodox church in the center of the city. My daughter and I attended a Bible study for missionary women, and we bought flowers and planted them in the flower boxes on her balcony.

In short, we experienced life as our daughter and her husband were experiencing it, and it was humbling, heart opening, and reassuring.

Time with Grandchildren

Our second trip to Bosnia was more than four years later, in late fall. Our daughter and son-in-law were parents now. Our first grandchild was born the previous summer, and we had enjoyed having him in our home for his first two months of life. Two more months had gone by, and we were anxious to see and connect with him again.

What a delight to hold him and cuddle him, to laugh with him and read him books, to dress him and change him, to put him to bed, and to remark over how much he'd grown and changed. How fun to watch him change even more the two weeks of our visit—to see him roll over by himself for the first time, begin to reach for and grab things, and begin to put weight on his legs when we held him in a standing position on our laps.

We felt such a connection to this wonderful child when he left with his parents to go back to the field. That connection grew even stronger on this visit, and we prayed that Solomon would remember us and feel a connection to us when he saw us again. (He did!) As he grows, we want him to know that we cared enough to be involved in his life overseas.

A Greater Vision

Several benefits come from being able to see in your mind, because you have been there yourself, the people, places, and activities your missionary talks and writes about. One benefit is that you can participate much more, through conversation and e-mail, in what your missionary is experiencing. John wrote of a visit to his daughter and her family on the field: "Our several-week visit centered on meeting people who are part of their everyday lives and going to places that are part of their everyday journey. Now, when they speak of someone or going to a certain place, we can picture it and add to the conversation, knowing who or what they are talking about. It gives us comfort to be able to do that."

A second benefit is being able to pray more specifically. Karen traveled with her husband and seventeen-year-old grandson to Vanuatu, an island country off the coast of Australia, to vacation in Port-Vila with her missionary son, his wife, and four grandchildren. Because of his work commitments, Karen's husband returned home, but Karen and her grandson went with her son's family to their home on the island of Tanna for another two weeks. "I wanted to live with them in their house," she said, "and get to know the people. I felt if I stayed this long that I would know how they live, I would know how to pray more effectively for them, and I could get to know the people so that I could pray for them. . . . We had time to eat all kinds of different foods, and to experience what happens when the water quits running." When you see your missionary's work up close, it's easier to empathize and to know how to pray.

Being on the field will almost certainly increase your desire to see the gospel made known around the world. "What an experience it was to attend worship where no one was speaking English," wrote John. He continued:

> It was very moving to stand and sing a familiar hymn in English while everyone around us was singing in Mandarin! [On our trip] we learned a great deal about the people and their history, and we have come home hungry to learn more. . . . We are certain that God is good. And Jesus is visible, even in a city with very few Christians, halfway around the world. The Good News is spreading like wildfire—we realize that we have a responsibility here at home to continue that growth while our children are helping to feed that growth in another country. God is everywhere and expects all of us to make His Son visible.

Encouragement for the Missionary

Visiting our missionary children speaks to them in ways we

might not have considered. Delaina, a missionary, expressed the value of parental visits this way:

> Visits from my mom and aunt and stepdad have been really special. It says that they are supportive of what I'm called to do and that they understand that my life . . . is here, that our relationship is not just a one-way road for me to travel back the thousands of miles it takes to get "home" to see them. It also allows them to see for themselves many of the things I've tried to or wanted to explain about my newfound homeland but just couldn't adequately express with just words. Also, their interaction with my friends and contacts has opened new doors to share the gospel that we might not have seen without their special visits.

Barbara wrote about the impact on the local people in her community because of her mother's visits: "My mother came three times to India and two times with me on a mission trip to Africa. . . . It helped to have my mother come because both places, India and Africa, are so family based, and it helped for people to see that even though I am fifty and single, I am not alone but have a family that cares for me and that I care for my family. That is very important here. And everywhere, everybody loved my mother."

Missionaries are also encouraged by the support they receive because of their parents' ability to communicate more effectively about the ministry when they return home. Barbara's mother is a good example of this. Barbara wrote:

> She saw how I was living, much more simply than most people back home, even though for my country it was pretty good. She got to know my staff members and the children we were working with, and she became a great advocate for me and my ministry back home. She has been raising sponsors, and she basically just tells about the things she saw and experienced in a way that is much closer to the people at home. She is still shocked about things that I now take for granted as normal happenings, and she is talking about them back home. So people get prayer requests for me and the ministry through her.

My son-in-law says that visits from parents "make the whole world a lot smaller. . . . It's really important that parents understand the calling and feel a part of the calling. Family is the first to send out. You can talk about the sending church and the missionaries, but really the family is the most primary part of sending, so they really need to buy into the vision. So visiting, meeting people, and seeing what's happening has been really helpful."

As we noted in chapter 1, our children desire our blessing as they become adults. That longing doesn't go away. Jim wrote, "One of the saddest comments I heard was from a missionary friend of our daughter. She thanked me for coming to see my daughter and sadly said, 'We have been here for many years, and neither of our parents have ever visited.' One set of parents did have health issues, but the other set traveled to many luxury-type places without ever making the effort to see their daughter and her family."

A missionary whose own parents were never able to visit her was encouraged when her husband's mother and stepfather made the trip once before the stepfather's death. "They had a good time," she wrote. "They went into China with us, and we got to show them a lot of the sights of Hong Kong as well. My husband's mom still talks about that trip and all she learned while here. We really appreciated their visit. They were here for two weeks, and it wasn't nearly long enough!" She also said, "I don't think [my] mom and dad ever really understood much about our work. I wish they could have seen for themselves what we do and how God takes care of us."

What to Know Before You Go

Okay, you're convinced. You'll go. Good!

If you've been invited to come, let your missionary know you accept. If a visit hasn't been discussed yet, tell your son or daughter that you'd like to come and are starting to make plans. Ask them about convenient dates to visit.

As you set your travel dates, keep in mind that the time of year you fly can dramatically affect ticket costs. Peak travel times to a certain area are always the most expensive. Even if you book tickets online yourself, it's worth a call to the airline's ticket office to ask about the least expensive time of year to fly to your destination.

Finding and Paying for Tickets

If you're comfortable working online, you might find and book flights yourself, and sometimes this saves you money. If you'd rather use a travel agency, consider finding one that specializes in serving missionaries and their families. Some agents offer to be available around the clock when you call from anywhere in the world in case you experience delays or other problems with connecting flights. Others promise low fares. Do an online search to find travel agencies that serve missions families and ask your missionary's sending organization or your church's missions ministry for referrals. Be sure to compare each agency's services; then choose what's best for you.

If you're using a frequent-flier program to pay for your tickets, the dates you fly can be even more important. It's much easier to get a free ticket during the off-season. The best times to redeem miles, according to the publisher of FrequentFlier. com, are 330 days before you travel (which is when carriers open their ticket inventories to frequent fliers) and two to three weeks before your departing date.[1] You won't want to disappoint your missionary or yourself by failing to get a last-minute ticket, so plan to book your flights early.

If you aren't using frequent-flier miles, paying for your flights may seem an overwhelming impossibility. Don't be afraid to ask your church for financial help if you need it. Missions-minded churches often have a fund set aside for unexpected expenses. Other churches might want to allow members to contribute to a special POM travel fund. One POM wrote, "We would encourage POMs to visit their children on the field if at all possible. We would encourage churches to help finance those visits, if needed. We went to see our children and grandchildren and wanted to come back and share with our church families who support them financially and in prayer." Getting parents of missionaries to the field is a win-win situation for everyone.

"If God ordains a trip, He will provide," wrote Sherrie Johnson in *Homefront Heartbeats*. She noted the gold, frankincense, and myrrh presented to Jesus shortly before Joseph was instructed to flee to Egypt with Mary and Jesus, the clothing and jewelry the Egyptians gave their Israelite neighbors just before the exodus, and the gifts and offerings given to the Jewish exiles who were preparing to return to Jerusalem to rebuild the temple. "If God is prompting you to consider a trip overseas," she wrote, "you can trust Him for the needed provisions. Ask Him."[2]

Passport Protocol

Most countries require travelers wanting to enter to hold a valid passport from the traveler's home country; a tourist visa may also be required, usually depending on the length of your stay. Your missionary should be able to tell you what you will need. The U.S. State Department offers Country Specific Information pages (formerly Consular Information Sheets) on its website with visa information, country by country. Go to www.travel. state.gov/travel and follow the links to access the CSI for your destination.

If you already have a passport, check the expiration date. Some countries require your passport to be valid for six months beyond the time you enter their borders. If you need to renew your passport or apply for a passport for the first time, be sure to allow plenty of time for processing. You should be able to locate passport information for your location on the Internet.

Medical and Travel Insurance

Check with your health insurance company to find out what international coverage, if any, your policy provides. Be aware that even if your policy covers you while overseas, you'll be required to pay all costs while you are overseas in order to receive services; your insurance company at home may then reimburse you for covered expenses. Also, ask your provider about medical evacuation coverage.

You may want to consider purchasing a short-term health insurance policy designed specifically to cover travel. Many travels agents and private companies offer such plans.

Some policies combine medical coverage with coverage for travel problems as well, such as lost baggage or cancelled flights. Read the fine print, and search for the policy that best fits your needs.

Other Health Precautions

Keep prescription medications in their original containers, clearly labeled. Be sure you have enough for the length of your trip. You may want to ask the foreign consulate of the country you will be visiting if any of your prescriptions are considered illegal substances in that country.

Pack all prescription medications in your carry-on luggage.

For extra security, pack a backup supply in your checked bags.

Consider carrying a letter from your doctor explaining your medical conditions, a list of all prescribed medications, and the generic names of your prescriptions. If you have any allergies that cause severe reactions, ask your doctor to include the specific treatment to follow in case you become ill. Wearing a medical alert bracelet is also wise. Pack any treatments you may need for common upsets such as diarrhea and vomiting.

If you wear glasses, take an extra pair in your carry-on.

You'll also want to find out what vaccinations, if any, are required or suggested for the area of the world you will visit. The Centers for Disease Control and Prevention (CDC) website offers information you may find helpful to share with your healthcare provider. Vaccinations are considered routine, recommended, or required. Plan early to get any immunizations that may be needed and the necessary documentation. See the CDC website at wwwn.cdc.gov/travel/contentVaccinations.aspx.

Last, be as physically fit as you can be before leaving on your overseas adventure. Being fit can help prevent illnesses and injuries and gives you stamina as you travel and during your visit.

Pack Wisely

Try to pack lightly. One of your checked bags is likely to be filled with supplies and gifts for your missionary's family, anyway! Plan to dress conservatively—nothing too flashy that would call attention to yourself and nothing too casual that would be offensive in some parts of the world. Plan to mix and match and to wear clothing items more than once. Packing light makes getting around easier, both in airports and on ground transportation. Use rolling luggage to save your back.

Keep your carry-on luggage light to make it easier to handle as well. A change of clothes, allowable limits of toiletries, prescription medications, and all your travel documents—that's all you really need.

Ask your missionary if you should bring gifts for those whose homes you will visit, and get suggestions for small gifts that will pack easily and travel well.

If you pack or carry any electronic devices—from computers to curling irons to digital cameras—pack the type of adaptor needed to plug those devices into the outlets in your hotel rooms or your missionary's home. Items that are less than five years old are likely to need only a "tip adaptor" to change the shape of the plug.[3]

Choose a camera that isn't too big, which can be cumbersome and can more clearly mark you to thieves as a target. Also consider wearing a money belt for carrying credit cards and cash.[4]

A notebook and a good pen (or your computer) are helpful for recording your experiences while you travel.

Flight Tips

You'll need to check in at the international ticket counter of your airline at least two hours before your flight. Check your bags all the way through to your final destination, unless you have an extremely long layover and will change airlines; that is when baggage is most likely to be lost.

You probably can't avoid jet lag altogether, but there are some ways you can minimize it. As soon as your flight is in the air, set your watch to the local time of your destination. If you're traveling east, and your flight leaves in the early evening, get to sleep as quickly as you can once dinner has been served. And if you can't sleep, try to convince your body that you did! That's what experienced traveler Doug Lucas, a missions mobilizer, advises. Brush your teeth, take off your shoes and put on some slippers, close your eyes (use a sleep mask too), and lie quietly. Ear plugs or noise-reducing earphones, a travel pillow, and an extra blanket can help too.[5]

When you're not sleeping on long flights, stay hydrated and get up and walk around from time to time. Flex your toes and rotate your ankles to help reduce swelling in your feet.

Know How to Fit In

People around the world behave differently from the people in your home country. Before you go, learn about the customs of the country you'll be visiting so you will be a welcomed guest.

Learn what style of dress is acceptable and arrive in that kind of clothing. Try to learn a few basic words in the country's language, and be willing to use them even if you feel foolish; if English is your native language, don't act as if you expect everyone you meet to understand you! If you're traveling to a developing country, learn how to eat and drink safely.

Ask your missionary about other customs you should follow. Usually it is not a good idea to use first names unless you are asked to, and don't photograph anyone without permission.

Keep a proper distance from others, and avoid long periods of eye contact. Know the local biases and prejudices and avoid giving offense in any way. Speak quietly. Don't spend conspicuously.

If your missionary works in a closed country, traveling to the field may not be possible. If you *are* able to visit, arming yourself with knowledge about appropriate behavior is even more important. You will not want to do or say anything that could indicate the religious nature of your missionary's work or the reason for your visit. Words such as *missions, missionary, evangelism, God, Jesus,* and *church* should never be spoken in any public place.

Encountering God

When you get to your destination and are reunited with your missionary, be prepared to experience some culture shock, even in your excitement and joy at this reunion. (As we described in chapter 8, culture shock is the feeling of having left comfort and familiarity behind and being surrounded by what is strange and different.) Keep an open heart, and follow your missionary's lead. In a story about her trip to Vanuatu to visit her son and his family in their village, Karen wrote:

> Erik and Michele try to get a taxi to help carry all the stuff that we have up to the village, but they cannot find one, so after much debate we decide to get as much stuff as we can into the truck and what we can't get in we will come back for later. So Erik loads box on top of box, and the suitcases go on top. We all climb into the truck. To my horror

the two boys [Karen's grandsons] climb on top of all of the boxes. Now, I am a city grandma who keeps the seatbelt and air bag laws to the letter, no compromise, so this does not bode well with me. Twice I hang out the window and yell at the boys to PLLEEASE be careful before I finally get a grip and pray about it. I am not in the USA, I remind myself. Go with the flow, grandma.

Sharing in the Work

Will you be assisting your missionary with his or her work while you are visiting? Polly did. When she and her husband stayed in Hungary with their grandchildren while her son and his wife traveled to meetings in Hong Kong, Polly led two out-reach quilting classes at the invitation of her son's teammate. She prepared twenty kits of fabric and patterns to give to the women in the classes and gave instructions through a translator.

At the end of each session, she talked about her life and shared her testimony. "Most of the ladies who attend our out-reaches are not believers," said the teammate who invited Polly to lead the sessions, "so our devotional time is always special as we try to reach these ladies with the message of God's love for them. They all really connected with Polly because they were able to view her as just like them—she is not a missionary, she is just a regular person who came to visit her family and loves to quilt."[6]

Lynn, a former missionary and now a POM, wrote about

the impact of her parents' travel to Japan:

> Spring 1981. We were missionaries in Tokyo and had just sent home a crew of volunteer builders from the U.S. In two-and-a-half weeks, they had managed to construct our new house/campus ministry building from the foundation stage to the under-roof stage.
>
> My parents, Hubert and Sadie Evelyn Lusby, then age sixty-one, were set to arrive for five weeks to help a follow-up crew do the inside finish work. Neither parent flies well. So the long flight they endured was even more remarkable given that this was their second visit—they well knew how hard the trip from Kentucky would be.
>
> Dad, a professional house painter, carpenter, and kitchen cabinet installer, set to work. One of the most unexpected moments came the day he met the Japanese tile man. Turns out, both had been young soldiers in WW II—Dad training to be a tail-gunner on the B-29; Mr. Narahashi training to be a Zero fighter pilot. But just as both were due to be sent out, the war ended. Now, brought together by this project, they were stunned with the awareness of what might have been. They looked into each other's eyes for a long, silent moment . . . and then melted into much bowing and hand-shaking.
>
> Mom was perfectly at home doing nonstop cooking, laundry, dishes, and entertaining the

grandchildren. Being a big talker, though, she was out of her element in the Japanese neighborhood where she had no way to communicate. One day she needed to get to the building site. It was finally decided that our Karis, only eight but fluent in Japanese, would escort her granny on the city bus. Mom must have felt very intimidated, especially after they were on their way and Karis told her, "I've never ridden the bus by myself before. Well . . . you're here, but you don't know anything."

My parents, who had never lived outside a twenty-mile radius in Kentucky, came halfway around the world because they knew the Lord wanted them to. They gave much and received a treasured, life-changing experience. Several Japanese friends continue to keep in touch with them and have visited their old Kentucky home. And for us . . . words can't describe what it meant to have them working beside us. And afterwards, daily seeing Mom and Dad's handiwork in that building was almost like having them there.

You might be asked to help with a building project, to work with children, or to participate in a conference. "God will use you in ways you never thought He would!" wrote Normalee Lucas in *Homefront Heartbeats*. She added, "Need I mention the importance of being careful not to criticize anything or to make too many 'suggestions' while you are there?"[7] Remember that your missionary is the one in charge when you are visiting.

Simply Being There Can Be Enough

It may be that your missionary doesn't need your help with any work but simply desires your presence and for you to experience what his or her life is like on the field. Bonnie wrote:

> Our first visit to France to see our son was one year after he left. He had been in language school for that year so we knew we would have a translator then! We had a wonderful time in Paris, just walking where he walked and seeing how life was in his very tiny apartment. We were able to take a road trip to Normandy and a fast train ride to southern France to visit some other missionaries. . . . We have also visited him during his internship in a church and were able to see and hear him preach, although we understood none of it. We did get the idea that he was talking about us when he looked at us, smiling and talking, and then the people all looked at us and laughed! Again he took us on a road trip to see the sights. Our favorite times were spent just drinking coffee and chatting and visiting with other missionaries. It is truly a blessing to spend time with our son in his corner of the world.

Like Bonnie, you'll find that participating in your missionary's normal life in this way is a powerful experience of seeing God at work.

Memories as Reminders

Some POMs like to record their experiences to share with others at home. Whether on video or on paper, this kind of sharing definitely helps friends and family who support your missionary experience what God is doing.

I sit writing the close to this chapter on the very day my daughter and son-in-law and my new grandson are *leaving* the field to reenter life here in their home country. Just two months ago, my husband and I visited them on the field, none of us knowing at the time that God would be bringing them home so soon. We are so grateful to have made our second visit when we did! We lived their life with them for two weeks; we spent time with people in their city they came to love and be loved by; we saw again the impact they had in their city and the tremendous need that still remains. Our visit brought us closer as a family, and our strong, clear memories of our trip remind us daily of the deep needs in the world and the only One able to meet them.

FROM SURVIVING TO THRIVIING

The POM journey can lead to good places,
if we are willing.

FINDING AND GIVING HELP

From Surviving to Thriving

Thanks for all your efforts on behalf of all of us POMs out here in the midst of nowhere, with no one to turn to who understands.

—a POM mom

The words of the POM quoted above speak to the heart and purpose of the ministry to parents of missionaries that Diane and I (Cheryl) work to promote. Too many POMs feel stranded in the middle of nowhere with no one who understands. We want to change that!

We consider our opportunity to raise the visibility of POM issues a privilege. However, we want to do more than raise awareness. We want to encourage action steps to help POMs not just survive their experience but thrive in their role while staying connected to distant loved ones. That has been the purpose of every chapter in this book. In this chapter, we want to focus even more on the importance of POMs finding help for themselves and offering help to others.

Reach Out!

POMs can do much to help ensure they successfully adjust to having adult children and grandchildren on a distant mission field. God never meant for us to cope with life's hardships alone. He knows we do better with help. He plans for us to have it.

However, we can thwart His plans by adopting cultural attitudes that admire independence and self-reliance. We make a mistake when we say things like, "God helps those who help themselves." In fact, God helps those who ask for help from Him and others! Ask God to show you if you've tried to remain too private and too independent and if you've kept Him from unfolding His plan in your life.

Let God Help

We have emphasized throughout this book the importance of talking to God about how we feel. Seek His comfort when you feel distressed. Some POMs hesitate to cast their cares upon God because they feel ashamed of their own emotions. This keeps them from enjoying the relief and freedom He wants to offer.

Do not feel ashamed of wishing your loved ones lived near. Separation from your family hurts because you love your children and grandchildren. Your love reflects God's parental love for us, His children. He wants us close to Him and actively seeks to draw us near to Him (John 12:32). You will fare better if you recognize your pain as natural, unavoidable, and understandable. God cares about your pain and waits to help you (Psalm 34:17).

In addition to casting your cares upon Him, we encourage you to don the full armor of God (Ephesians 6:11) each day by meditating on His goodness and promises, seeking Him in His Word, and talking with Him in prayer. Satan lurks about waiting for a chance to bring you down. He has a greater chance of succeeding when you feel stressed and upset. Don't engage the battle without securing your defense.

Let Others Help

While POMs can do many things to help themselves, they fare better when they receive eager help from caring others. As Betty Jo put it, "Parents who receive support are less likely to hinder their children than those without it."

Help from Other POMs. As a POM, you need safe confidantes to talk with. Even Adam, who walked closely and personally with God in the perfect conditions of the garden of Eden, needed human intimacy and companionship (Genesis 2:18). You too need a personal support team of people you can talk with candidly.

Your support team could include caring family members, empathic friends, pastors, or even a professional counselor. Don't go it alone. Bearing one another's burdens is commanded in Scripture. You have an extraordinary burden to bear—give someone else the privilege of helping you carry it! (If you find you only feel worse about yourself after talking with others, you may need help discriminating between safe and unsafe people. We recommend the book *Safe People* by Dr. Henry Cloud and Dr. John Townsend for help in this area.)

You may enjoy meeting other POMs who fully understand your feelings and needs. Some POMs meet casually as friends; others form structured groups. Laura found it helpful to connect with others who understood her experience: "We met with two couples Friday night—wonderful, wonderful people! One couple just found out their first grandchild will be born on the field and are having a real hard time with that. It was good to know that our emotions, feelings, and thoughts are so very, very normal."

I (Diane) greatly appreciated my early POM support-group experience. I wrote in our church newsletter: "The parent group provided a place for my true feelings to be heard and understood by others whose experiences were similar to mine. We listened to one another, cried together, and encouraged each other and ourselves. Progress was sometimes slow!" Later, when our group expanded, a meeting came just days before our daughter and son-in-law's furlough ended. Just being with other POMs that night filled me up emotionally and made the departure a little easier to face.

Help from Your Missionary. Let your missionary know what would be most helpful to you. We believe God wants missionaries and their parents to function as a family unit despite the mission and the miles. We encourage you to ask for and expect your missionary to make time for long-distance contacts with you and to reserve time for you during furloughs. While POMs naturally want to do everything possible to support their missionary, we believe relationships should work both ways. Interpersonal arrangements that allow most or all the care to flow one way amount to ministries, not relationships. Jesus taught us to "love *one another*" (John 13:34, italics added), and Paul told us to "bear *one another's* burdens" (Galatians 6:2, italics added).

Help from Your Church. We have heard some wonderful stories about churches that recognize the needs of POMs. Churches have sent youth groups to help POMs with fall leaf raking and they have recognized POMs in the congregation on Mother's Day and Father's Day. Churches have hosted dinners to honor POMs and provided funds or frequent-flier miles for travel to the field or to bring missionaries home for family emergencies.

Maybe you can help your church start a POM group in your area. We would be happy to assist; see the NNPOM contact information at the back of this book.

Share What You've Learned

As you adjust and learn to thrive as a POM, you gain valuable wisdom and experience and sharing what you've learned can help others involved in the cause of world missions.

Mentor Other POMs

Experienced POMs can effectively mentor new POMs and the parents of missionary recruits. David and Donna learned this when they joined a POM group while their daughter, Lydia, was doing a six-month internship in Africa. "The mixture of veteran and new POMs was great for us," Donna explained. She continued:

> They understood what we were headed for, the good and the bad. They were accepting of us and willing to share their experiences and heartaches in areas we had not yet thought through. We gained good ideas in practical things too, such as communicating by computer, shipping things overseas, and what to do on holidays. The fellowship, encouragement, and support keep us going. Sharing a meal and stories together with people who have already walked this path builds relationships, which is important to us.

At a missions convention recently, I (Diane) walked up and down the aisles where people were gathering in the main arena. I wanted to invite POMs to a special event being held for them at the convention the next day. "Do you know any parents of missionaries?" I asked those I saw. One woman said, "Yes, me." When I gave her a flyer about the POM event, tears instantly filled her eyes. Reaching out to POMs who are hurting is one way I share what I have learned.

Be an Advocate for Families

POMs can advocate for missions practices that help families create and maintain strong bonds across the miles. If you felt blindsided by your child's decision to become a missionary, take advantage of opportunities you have to speak up about that. Talk to recruits as well as to representatives of colleges and sending organizations about the stress recruits cause when they keep their parents in the dark during such a major decision-making process. Perhaps you can speak to some of your congregation's leaders about ways your church can offer support to you and other POMs in your area.

Worrying about parents and unresolved relationship issues can keep potential recruits from going to the field. Worrying can impair the work of missionaries as they serve and can even cause some to return from the field prematurely. Writing in *World Christian,* Eolene Boyd quoted Don Boesel, who said, "Guilt can eat away at the energy of a missionary and immobilize him."[1] We think anyone with an interest in furthering world missions should also have an interest in helping POMs adjust well to the career decisions made by their adult children.

Look to the Future

After you have secured support from God and others, you can begin taking charge in your own life and doing things that will help you survive and thrive as a POM. Every day, the decisions you make about self-worth, self-care, use of time, companionship, and activities shape the way the rest of your personal story will unfold. Decide now to take charge in your life and "write" an upbeat life story.

Yes, you need to grieve; we hope we've been clear about that. But that's only half the story. You need to both grieve and change what you can in your life. Make decisions that move you toward fullness of life even though your missionary lives far away. What does God want to do with the rest of *your* life? Jim entered mission service himself after becoming a POM: "My children are serving Him," he said. "Their steps of faith influenced me to boldly move forward to serve the Lord." The Finishers Project (www.finishers.org) can help you learn about short-term and second-career ministry projects that might fit you.

See Yourself as We See You

If you're a POM, please look in the mirror and see yourself through our eyes as someone who has made a blessed sacrifice for the kingdom and someone God wants to use in unforeseen ways in days to come. You struggle because you love. Accept your feelings. Ask for and accept help from God, from your missionary, and from friends, churches, and other sending organizations. And do all you can to help yourself.

Diane and I know of few writers who have focused attention on the positive contribution POMs make to missions. We applaud those who have.

Eddie Gibbs gave early recognition to the special experience and needs of POMs. Writing to missionaries in *World Christian* in 1996, he said: "Parents face more of the costs of missionary service than their children. You've got the adventure; you get to go to new places. But your parents are left behind, with your photograph over the fireplace. The Lord may assess their contribution as greater than yours."[2]

In 1998, Norman Miller recognized in *Church Administration* that POMs "give away a part of themselves, leaving a family-sized void."[3] And in 2003, Scott R. Johnson, writing for crosswalk.com, noted that "little is said about the sacrifices of those left behind. . . . It requires that they release their loved ones into God's hands in a way they may never have done before. Sometimes it requires the release of hopes and dreams."[4] He related the comment of one missionary who acknowledged, "My mom had always dreamed of my being married, having children and living close by, sharing all those experiences with me."[5]

We hope you catch our vision now and join us in thinking of the POM experience as a dangerous opportunity. We think that when parents, missionaries, and mission leaders work together according to God's plan, POMs can avoid the risk of getting stuck in grief and can expect their journey to end in a good place. Accept the help and validation offered by God and others, learn more about yourself and God's faithfulness, heal past injuries, strengthen marital and family bonds, and stretch to live in a broader and more exciting world.

Sensing God at work, Rhonda wrote, "I wonder where this will take us in our walk with Christ . . . how it will change me." We invite you to recognize with us that God will use your experience to change you and finally enable you to say with the psalmist, "He makes my feet like hinds' feet, and sets me upon my high places" (Psalm 18:33).

NOTES

Chapter 1, This Isn't Easy

1. John Trent and Gary Smalley, *The Blessing*, rev. ed. (1993; Nashville: Thomas Nelson, 2004), 30.

2. Rose Roberts, "A Word of Encouragement from a Missionary Daughter," *Harvest Legacy*, Spring 2005, <http://www.womenoftheharvest.com/legacy/apr05.htm>.

Chapter 2, Something Must Be Wrong with Me

1. C. S. Lewis, *A Grief Observed* (San Francisco: Harper, 1961), 5.

Chapter 4, Do I Know You?

1. Jeanette and Robert Lauer, *How to Survive and Thrive in an Empty Nest: Reclaiming Your Life When Your Children Have Grown* (Oakland, CA: New Harbinger Publications, 1999), 19.

2. Melissa M. Ahern and Michael S. Hendryx, "Social Capital and Risk for Chronic Illness," *Chronic Illness*, September 2005, (1:3), 183–190.

3. Tim Alan Gardner, *Sacred Sex: A Spiritual Celebration of Oneness in Marriage* (Colorado Springs: WaterBrook Press, 2002), 44.

4. Robert Browning, *Rabbi Ben Ezra,* 1862, <http://www.theotherpages.org/poems/brown01.html#7>.

Chapter 5, Almost More Than I Can Take

1. U.S. Census Bureau, 2006 American Community Survey, <http://www.factfinder.census.gov>.

2. Susan Miller, *After the Boxes Are Unpacked* (Wheaton: Tyndale House, 1998), 28.

Chapter 6, Saying Good-Bye Well

1. Norman J. P., "Being Effective on the Field," *Momentum,* January/ February 2007, 18, <http://www.momentum-mag.org>.

2. Mr. and Mrs. Roger Robinson, quoted in "What Other Parents Are Saying," <http://www.joinus.campuscrusadeforchrist.com/Parents/ otherparents.htm>.

Chapter 7, One More Hug

1. David Crim, "Letting Go," <http://www.thetask.org/students/Info/ lettinggo.htm>.

2. Dave Sprinkle, panel discussion, 2006 National Missionary Convention workshop "How Do I Help Them Understand?"

Chapter 8, Different Isn't Always Wrong

1. Patricia Magness, "Energy, Urgency, and Excitement in Missions Today," *Christian Standard,* February 11, 2007, 88–89.

2. <http://www.uscwm.org/>.

3. <http://www.createinternational.com/index. php?site=thechallenge>.

4. Ibid.

5. Heidi Long, "Confessions of a Reluctant Missionary," *Momentum,* January/February 2007, 89, <http://www.momentum-mag.org>.

6. Ronald L. Koteskey, "What Missionaries Ought to Know About Culture Stress," <http://www.missionarycare.com/brochures/br_culturestress.htm>.

7. B. Van Ochs (pseudonym), "Ten Challenges That May Make Staying Home Look Attractive," *Evangelical Missions Quarterly,* April 2005, <https://bgc.gospelcom.net/emquonline/emq_article_read_pv.php?ArticleID=3440>.

8. Marti Smith, *Through Her Eyes: Life and Ministry of Women in the Muslim World* (Waynesboro, GA: Authentic Media, 2004), 160.

9. Adrian Fehl, "The Lesson and Life," *The Lookout,* July 18, 2004, 11.

10. "Going Home," <http://www.peterswife.org/PWArchive.php?Show=GoingHome>.

11. Van Ochs, "Ten Challenges That May Make Staying Home Look Attractive."

12. John and Diane Larsen, "Third Culture Kids: Expatriate Children," <http://www.home.snu.edu/~hculbert/tck.htm>.

13. "MK—Fit In or Misfit?" <http://www.peterswife.org/PWArchive.php?Show=FitInOrMisfit>.

14. Ibid.

15. "Long Distance Grandmothering," <http://www.peterswife.org/PWArchive.php?Show=Grandmothering>.

16. Joy, "Breaking Free," *Women of the Harvest Online eMagazine,* November/December 2007 <https://www.womenoftheharvest.com/publications_home.asp>.

17. Robert R. Recker, "The Challenges of Missionary Life, Part IV," *Missionary Monthly,* December 1, 1996, 12–13.

18. Parent-to-Parent, *Harvest Legacy,* 1:3.

Chapter 9, Together Again

1. Ronald L. Koteskey, "What Missionaries Ought to Know about Re-Entry," <http://www.missionarycare.com/brochures/br_reentry.htm>.

2. <http://www.peterswife.org/PWArchive.php?Show=GoingHome>.

3. Neal Pirolo, *Sending as Servers* (San Diego: Emmaus Road, International; Wheaton: ACMC, 1991), 139–146.

4. Edward and Linda Speyers, *65 Ways to Love and Encourage Missionaries* (Holland, MI; self-published booklet, 2001), 40. Contact the authors: ed_speyers@wycliffe.org.

5. Mariana Nesbitt, "Making Home Furloughs Easier," <http://www.strategicnetwork.org/index.php?loc=kb&>.

6. Paula Cowan, "Emotional Support for Furlough," *Harvest Legacy,* Spring 2005, <https://www.womenoftheharvest.com/publications_home.asp>.

7. David Crim, "Letting Go," <http://www.thetask.org/students/Info/lettinggo.htm>.

Chapter 10, A Piece of Myself

1. Dr. Richardson shared her insights with me in conversation in September 2007.

2. Selma Wassermann, *The Long Distance Grandmother,* fourth ed. (Vancouver, BC: Harley & Marks, 2001), 5.

3. Sherrie Johnson, "Praying for Your Grandchildren," *Homefront Heartbeats,* Summer 2006, 3.

4. <http://www.grandparentinggreat.com>.

Chapter 12, High-Tech and No-Tech Ways to Stay Close

1. Mary Hunt, "The 411 on International Phone Calls," *Everyday Cheapskate* e-mail, September 18, 2007, <http://www.everydaycheapskate.com>.

2. Marty Andry, Doug Lucas, and Chris Bushnell, *Resources for Missionary Recruits Online, Appendix C: Writing to Christian Workers in Creative Access Countries,* <http://www.teamexpansion.org/resources/recruitguide/resomrAppendixC.htm>.

Chapter 13, The World Is My Neighborhood

1. Jane L. Levere, "Take 'Em for a Ride," AARP, March/April 2005, 17.

2. Sherrie Johnson, "God Provides Before the Need," *Homefront Heartbeats,* Summer 2004, 2.

3. Doug Lucas, "Cool Tools for Travel & Missions," <http://www.brigada.org/brigade/?p=15>, compiled from *Brigada Today,* <http://www.brigada.org>.

4. Ibid.

5. Ibid.

6. Patti Humphry, "Appreciating Polly Hiltibran," *Homefront Heartbeats,* Summer 2006, 2.

7. Normalee Lucas, "Reflections of a Missionary Parent," *Homefront Heartbeats,* Summer 2005, 4.

Chapter 14, Finding and Giving Help

1. Eolene Boyd, "Agencies: What Does Honor Mean?" *World Christian,* January/February 1996, 22.

2. Eddie Gibbs, "When God Says Go! and They Say No!" *World Christian,* March/April 1996, 21.

3. Norman Miller, "Ministering to Parents of Missionaries," *Church Administration,* January 1998, 12.

4. Scott Johnson, "Family Support: The Special Role Parents Play in Missions," <http://www.crosswalk.com/1197165/>, April 2003.

5. Ibid.

RESOURCES FOR POMS

Books Related to Missions

On Being a Missionary, Thomas Hale, William Carey Library
Publishers, 2003.

Operation World, Patrick Johnstone, Authentic, 2001.

Perspectives on the World Christian Movement, edited by Ralph D.
Winter, William Carey Library Publishers, 1999.

Scaling the Wall, Kathy Hicks, Authentic, 2003.

Serving as Senders, Neal Pirolo, Emmaus Road International, 1991.

Through Her Eyes, Marti Smith, Authentic, 2004.

Third Culture Kids, David C. Pollock and Ruth E. Van Reken,
Nicholas Brealey Publishing, 2001.

Books Related to Relationships

The Blessing, John Trent, PhD, and Gary Smalley, Thomas Nelson,
2004.

Boundaries, Dr. Henry Cloud and Dr. John Townsend, Zondervan,
2002.

Boundaries in Marriage, Dr. Henry Cloud and Dr. John Townsend,
Zondervan, 2002.

Grandma, I Need Your Prayers, Quin Sherrer and Ruthanne Garlock,
Zondervan, 2002.

How to Have That Difficult Conversation You've Been Avoiding, Dr.

Henry Cloud and Dr. John Townsend, Zondervan, 2006.

Living the Lois Legacy, Helen Kooiman Hosier, Tyndale, 2002.

The Long Distance Grandmother, fourth edition, Selma Wassermann, Hartley and Marks Publishers, 2001.

Long Distance Grandma, Janet Tietsort, Howard Books, 2005.

Sacred Sex, Tim Alan Gardner, Waterbrook, 2002.

Safe People, Dr. Henry Cloud and Dr. John Townsend, Zondervan, 1996.

The Second Half of Marriage, David and Claudia Arp, Zondervan, 2000.

Newsletters and Other Publications

Brigada Today, <http://www.brigada.org>

Evangelical Missions Quarterly, <http://www.emqonline.com/>

Harvest Legacy,
    <https://www.womenoftheharvest.com/publications_home.asp>

Homefront Heartbeats,
    <http://equip.efca.org/course/caringformissionaries>

Missions Catalyst e-Magazine, <http://www.missionscatalyst.org>

Mission Frontiers, <http://www.missionfrontiers.org/>

NNPOM e-newsletter, <http://www.pomnet.org>

Women of the Harvest (for missionary women),
    <https://www.womenoftheharvest.com/publications_home.asp>

Websites and Organizations

ASSIST News Service, <http://www.assistnews.net>

Finishers Project, <http://www.finishers.org/>

Grandparenting Great, <http://www.grandparentinggreat.com>

MisLinks, <http://www.mislinks.org/>

Missionary Care: Resources for Missions and Mental Health,
    <http://www.missionarycare.com/>

Mission Network News, <http://www.mnnonline.org>

National Network of Parents of Missionaries,
    <http://www.pomnet.org>

US Center for World Missions, <http://www.uscwm.org/>

World Missions Atlas Project, <http://www.worldmap.org/>

PRAYING FOR YOUR MISSIONARY

●

Many other resources offer suggestions about how to pray for missionaries. Our list of prayer suggestions includes requests for the needs of your missionary as an individual and as part of an extended family.

1. Pray that your missionary's work succeeds according to God's plan.

2. Pray for boldness in witness and for open doors and open hearts.

3. Pray for the safety and well-being of your missionary family.

4. Pray for spiritual power and protection from Satan.

5. Pray for strong financial and personal support from sending organizations and friends.

6. Pray for harmonious and effective team and family relationships.

7. Pray that the importance of ministry does not cause your missionary to devalue or deny his or her own personal need for care in the form of space, consideration, rest, and love.

8. Pray that the importance of ministry does not cause your

missionary to devalue or deny the importance of extended family relationships.

9. Pray for healing and maturity in the growth areas you as a parent recognize.

10. Pray that all that is best about your own family culture will continue to give your missionary strength in his new, distant environment and culturally different community.

11. Pray that your missionary will be in tune with God's leading and able to resist external pressures to do something or be someone that does not fit well with who he is or her own special gifts.

12. Pray that your missionary will be able to love his or her spouse and raise your grandchildren with sensitivity, love, and validation, avoiding pride, legalism, workaholism, and rigidity.

PRAYING FOR YOURSELF AND OTHER POMS

Here's how you can pray for parents of missionaries, and how POMs can pray for themselves and other POMs too. Pray that POMs will:

1. Experience the comfort the Holy Spirit promises to those who need it.

2. Accept and support the missionary calling of their son or daughter.

3. Realize that their acceptance and support will strongly affect their son or daughter's happiness and effectiveness as a missionary.

4. Resolve any issues with their adult child and say good-bye well.

5. Know joy because God has chosen their son or daughter for a particular task and because their child has been obedient to God's call.

6. Establish and maintain frequent communication with their missionary son or daughter and his or her family.

7. Find a loving support group or network that understands and appreciates them.

8. Speak honestly with friends about their feelings and deal with their grief in healthy ways.

9. Take initiative and find ways to develop and maintain a connection with their grandchildren, even across the miles.

10. Consider seeking out other young people at home who need love, mentoring, and encouragement.

Adapted from an article by Gerald and June McNeely in *Parents as Partners,* a publication of the International Mission Board of the Southern Baptist Convention.

ACKNOWLEDGEMENTS

Judy Johnson—You said it first: "Help the parents."

Sherri Johnson and Cindy Blomquist—You encouraged and supported from the beginning.

Ellen Cook, PhD—You cared about underserved populations and supported POM research at the University of Cincinnati in 2005.

Greater Cincinnati Parents of Missionaries—You risked honesty with us and proved the power of the "one anothers" of the Bible.

"Pom-Pom Girls" (Alice, Cindy, Rhonda, Linda), Atlanta, Georgia—You met each other the same day you met us, and you blessed us many times over during the writing of this book.

Walter Birney and the National Missionary Convention—Thank you for supporting our efforts each year.

Wayne Shaw—Thank you for lunch, and thank you for your tears as you talked about missing your grandchildren overseas.

David Mays—You challenged us to persevere. We have.

LifeSpring Christian Church, Cincinnati, Ohio—Thank you for making it financially possible for us to launch a ministry to POMs.

Sheila and Scoggins Berg, Heidi and Doug Collins, Cindi and Mark Phipps—Your missionary spirits have emboldened us.

Dr. Vietta Keith Richardson, Sue and Dan Burton, Lynn Lusby Pratt—Thank you for sharing your expertise so willingly.

POMs who participated in Cheryl's doctoral research—You answered so many questions because you cared.

All the POMs and missionaries who wrote to us and prayed for us as we wrote—Ephesians 1:16. You have blessed us and everyone who reads this book.

ABOUT THE AUTHORS

Cheryl Savageau, EdD, is a professional clinical counselor who formerly served as director of counseling ministries at LifeSpring Christian Church in Cincinnati, Ohio. She also has served as visiting professor at Manila Bible Seminary and Baguio College of Ministry in the Philippines and Lakeview Bible College in Chennai, India. Cheryl's doctoral dissertation is entitled *An Ecological Analysis of the Stresses Experienced by Parents of Missionaries* (2005).

Mother of two adult children, Cheryl has worked as a Christian counselor since 1985, focusing primarily on marriage, parenting, and family counseling and helping people through loss and recovery. She resides with her husband, Charlie, in Greenville, South Carolina.

Diane Stortz, formerly editorial director for Standard Publishing in Cincinnati, Ohio, was a POM for five-and-a-half years. During that time she cofounded, along with Cheryl Savageau, the National Network of Parents of Missionaries (NNPOM) and a support group for POMs in the greater Cincinnati area. Diane graduated from Arizona State University with a bachelors degree in journalism. She is the author of *Jesus Loves You: A Read-the-Pictures Book* and a variety of Happy Day* Books (Standard Publishing). Now freelancing, she edits books for many publishers, and in 2010 Zonderkidz will publish a Bible storybook she has written. Visit Diane's website at www.izzysoffice.com.

Mother of two and grandmother of one, Diane continues to minister to POMs from her home in Cincinnati, where she lives with her husband, Ed.

ABOUT NNPOM

Founded in 2003 by coauthors Cheryl Savageau and Diane Stortz, the National Network of Parents of Missionaries is a nondenominational ministry dedicated to helping parents of missionaries connect with one another and learn to succeed and thrive as POMs. Our dream is to form local groups of POMs, provide resources and networking opportunities, and help churches and sending organizations provide care for the parents of their missionaries.

We've posted a variety of POM stories related to the subject of this book on our website, www.pomnet.org.